Genre and the City

This book's chapters analyze aspects of urban politics with a combination of critical thinking (influenced by Walter Benjamin, Jacques Ranciere, Henri Lefebvre, and Achille Mbembe, among others) and readings of artistic genres (film, literature, and architecture). The coverage of cities includes Tokyo, Paris, New York, Nairobi, Boston, Berlin and Hong Kong.

This book was published as a special issue of *Journal for Cultural Research*.

Michael J. Shapiro is a Professor of Political Science at the University of Hawaii. Among his recent publications are *Cinematice Geopolitics* (Routledge, 2009) and *The Time of the City: Politics, Philosophy and Genre* (Routledge 2010).

Genre and the City

Edited by
Michael J. Shapiro

LONDON AND NEW YORK

First published 2011
by Routledge
2 Park Square, Milton Park, Abingdon, Oxfordshire OX14 4RN

Simultaneously published in the USA and Canada
by Routledge
711 Third Avenue, New York, NY 10017

First issued in paperback 2014

Routledge is an imprint of the Taylor and Francis Group, an informa business

© 2011 Taylor & Francis

This book is a reproduction of *Journal for Cultural Research* 12.1. The Publisher requests to those authors who may be citing this book to state, also, the bibliographical details of the special issue on which the book was based.

Typeset in Times New Roman by Taylor & Francis Books

All rights reserved. No part of this book may be reprinted or reproduced or utilised in any form or by any electronic, mechanical, or other means, now known or hereafter invented, including photocopying and recording, or in any information storage or retrieval system, without permission in writing from the publishers.

British Library Cataloguing in Publication Data
A catalogue record for this book is available from the British Library

ISBN 978-0-415-61435-1 (hbk)

ISBN 978-1-138-88206-5 (pbk)

Disclaimer
The publisher would like to make readers aware that the chapters in this book are referred to as articles as they had been in the special issue. The publisher accepts responsibility for any inconsistencies that may have arisen in the course of preparing this volume for print.

Contents

Notes on Contributors   vii

1. **Introduction: Genre and the City**
   Michael J. Shapiro   1

2. **Genre and the City: Tokyo's Urban Space**
   Bettina Johanna Brown   3

3. **Policing Paris: Private Publics and Architectural Media in Michael Haneke's *Caché***
   Brianne Gallagher   19

4. **Crossing the Border: Art and Change in East Harlem**
   Allison Pan   39

5. **Genre and the African City: The Politics and Poetics of Urban Rhythms**
   Sam Okoth Opondo   59

6. **Centrifugal Bostons and Competing Imaginaries in *Mystic River***
   Nicolette Rowe   81

7. **Intercity Cinema: Hong Kong at the Berlinale**
   Michael J. Shapiro   99

Index   121

Notes on Contributors

Bettina Johanna Brown is a Ph.D. candidate in the Department of Political Science at the University of Hawaii at Manoa.

Brianne Gallagher is a Ph.D. candidate in the Department of Political Science at the University of Hawaii at Manoa.

Sam Okoth Opondo is a Ph.D. candidate in the Department of Political Science at the University of Hawaii at Manoa. His research centers on African poetics, cultural translation, and African modes of mediating estrangement.

Allison Pan is an MA candidate in the Department of Political Science at the University of Hawaii at Manoa. She is currently completing her thesis on international relations theory and contemporary global security challenges.

Nicolette Rowe has an MA in Political Science from the University of Hawaii at Manoa and is enrolled to begin law school in the fall of 2008 at the William S. Richardson School of Law.

Michael J. Shapiro is a Professor of Political Science at the University of Hawaii at Manoa. Among his recent publications is *Deforming American Political Thought: Ethnicity, Facticity and Genre* (University Press of Kentucky, 2006). His *Cinematic Geopolitics* is in press at Routledge.

Introduction: Genre and the City

Michael J. Shapiro

Two episodes created the occasions for the essays in this monograph issue of the *Journal for Cultural Research*. The first was the graduate research seminar on "Genre and the City" that I taught in the spring of 2007. This paragraph from the course syllabus tells much of the story:

> This seminar on "research methods" will be oriented by a concern with the politics of aesthetics and will feature a variety of genres aimed at illuminating urban life worlds. During the first half to two thirds of the course, we will — based on readings and visual materials — discuss the way the city can be understood by heeding architecture, crime fiction, film (noir among other genres), photography, painting, novels, television, and treatises on political economy. The latter part of the course will be devoted to student [writing] projects in which each student chooses a city and analyzes the way its political life can be discerned by focusing on alternative (at least two) genres.

The essays in this monograph by Bettina Brown, Brianne Gallagher, Allison Pan, Sam Opondo, and Nicolette Rowe are revised versions of the seminar papers they wrote for the course. As is evident from the content of the essays, the authors draw in large measure on the same pool of theoretical references — which constituted some of the course readings — while deploying them on different urban venues — Tokyo, Paris, New York, Nairobi, and Boston respectively.

The second episode was my attendance (during the period of the course) at the Berlinale, the 2007 Berlin Film Festival. Edified by some of the same theoretical references that inspired my students' essays, I wrote an essay on contemporary Hong Kong (understood in the context of contemporary Berlin), thus adding two cities to the mix. I am grateful to both those students whose essays are included in this monograph issue and others in the course, whose contributions to the seminar helped me to shape my own essay.

Genre and the City: Tokyo's Urban Space

Bettina Johanna Brown

By utilizing the locus of cinema's narrational space, Tokyo's urban world as political life is discerned by way of spatial, temporal and cultural practices within architectural and aesthetic contexts. Additional genres are employed as potential analytical and theoretical exposition.

Preface

Contemporary urban Tokyo contains multiple spatio-temporal layers, articulated by its architectural habitus as well as by various appropriated discourses as the city's contingent encounters unfold. In her film *Lost in Translation* (2003), Sofia Coppola exercises significant aspects of Tokyo's habitus. In one exemplary scene, a fire-drill sequence, hotel guests are awakened at an odd hour by an alarm and hustled to the proximity of the hotel's main entrance. The scene inverts domains of private versus public in a way that articulates with the spatial/temporal disorientation of the film's two main characters, Bob (Bill Murray) and Charlotte (Scarlett Johansson). In this scene, Charlotte looks at Bob, who is a few steps away and clothed in a *yukata* housecoat. He notices her white bedroom slippers contrasted against the asphalt; her hands stuffed in her pockets. In addition to their awkward ensembles, their shared vulnerabilities are also expressed by their awkward stances and facial expressions, which are inhibited by the immediacy of the night chill, and their past and present situational uncertainties.

This scene evokes a relevant sense-memory of Tokyo for me. As a child, sometimes sitting on my father's shoulders, I moved through miles of temple ground in Kyoto and Nara, the temples' rooflines reminding me of giant wings sheltering their inhabitants. I recall the quietness of the spaces we traversed; the most noticeable sound was the rhythmic crunching of gravel under our feet. The meticulously raked rock gardens, flowing as the sea, are among my initial memories of being a part of something much larger than myself, reflecting an architectural habitus and a trajectory of movement inflected by the built environment.

Akiko-san, my home caregiver, patiently molded my erratic childhood physicality into culturally acceptable modes of deliberate movement. We lived in Denenchofu, a residential district of Tokyo, in a traditional home furnished with *tatami* floor mats, *shoji* doors, *futon* mattresses, *zabuton* cushions and an *ofuro* hot tub. As my body adjusted to the spatial dimensions of these new surfaces, I learned to sit on bent knees, legs beneath me, hands folded in my lap. I opened *shoji* doors in a kneeling position, mediated clumsy motion in the mastery of chopsticks and danced in school performances with playful, coquettish movement. From a child's perspective, I began to recognize my body to be not only an agent of spatial negotiation, but also a form of haptic articulation. This purview introduces the following theoretical and analytical expositions of how bodies relate to space.

Introduction

Edified by the narrational space of the films *Lost in Translation* and *Babel*, and literary genres within aesthetic and architectural contexts, this article examines the interdependent relationships between self and other that are inflected by Tokyo's urban habitus, as local and exotic bodies seek to accommodate themselves within the city's practices and environment. My emphasis, which enacts a politics of aesthetics, is focused on the way architecture imposes practices on bodies and the ways in which the bodies themselves seek to extract a resistant individuality. The significance of this examination, as it seeks to discern Tokyo's urban world as political life, is that it reframes the debate and the ontological criteria by which the political within the urban is constructed and assessed.

My analysis resists traditional mimetic, representative narratives and inquiries aimed at their exposition, and prolongs the suspension of the analytical gap between perception and belief rather than seeking to effect its reconciliation. As a methodology of critical inquiry, its aim is to elucidate *how* we think about political life rather than to evoke the *what* of its definition. Put another way, the focus is on how power is experienced rather than on how it is exercised.

In what follows, two films, Sofia Coppola's *Lost in Translation* and Alejandro González Iñárritu's *Babel*, guide us through the inter- and intra-cinematic exposition of bodies in relation to space. In order to theorize my film readings, I invoke texts on architectural appropriations by Giuliana Bruno and Sergei M. Eisenstein, who provide insights into the relationship of architectural embodiment as it is expressed cinematically. I also turn to fiction and non-fiction genres, to the works of Haruki Murakami and Peter Carey respectively, who provide aesthetic, historical juxtapositions within Tokyo's urban milieu as experienced through the narratives of their primary characters. As a final reference, Walter Benjamin's historical rendering of the urban — of dweller to structure — is included.

Spatial/Temporal Practices: Appropriations of Architectural Space and Production

In *Lost in Translation*, Bob Harris is a man past his prime with regard to both his age and acting career. He travels to Tokyo to be featured in a Suntory whisky advertising spot. In the film's opening sequence, Bob awakens to the automatic opening of his hotel room curtains. Startled by the unexpected, he looks around for the mechanical source of the visual effect. He continues his bleary journey to the shower, attempts to adjust its height and submits to its limits in comical contortion. Subsequent contortions, mostly in the form of inhibitions in his bodily comportment, are evidenced by demands for innumerable bowing gestures and expectations of rigid interpersonal dissociation in crowded elevators. In addition, he is shown entrapped by high-speed exercise machines. Bob's disrupted comportment and biological rhythms establish the film's primary spatio-temporal narrative at the outset. Apart from what the characters experience, the film's depiction of potential ontological connections between protagonist and spectator embodiment mobilizes a shared *haptic space* — the embodied spaces of acting and viewing. The intelligibility of the film is a function of the sense memories of the viewers as they connect their experiences of maladjustment with those of the protagonist. As Giuliana Bruno (1997, p. 19) points out: "bodies in space design spatial fields, which in turn design corporealities". She adds "that by framing such views, they also frame spectatorial bodies" (p. 20). Sergei M. Eisenstein's (1989, p. 129) perspective on the role of architecture in the cinematic *mise en scène* articulates well with Bruno's insights. As Yve-Alain Bois puts it: "Eisenstein had to find practical answers to the problem of how to film a building, how to transform it, from a passive setting of the action, into a major agent of the plot" (Eisenstein 1989, p. 113). In *Lost in Translation*, viewers may perceive the structural dynamic in a way that is imperceptible to Bob. Within this perspective, architecture is an active participant in the shaping of experience. Its effect becomes evident as one moves within its compass:

> Where architectural interiors are concerned, one might adduce more "direct" examples, taken from other pages in the history of architecture, such as the system of rising vaults in Hagia Sophia, which reveal their scope and magnificence step by step, or the interplay of arcades and vaulting in Chartres Cathedral, whose calculated magic of sequential montage I have admired more than once. (Eisenstein 1989, p. 129)

As Bob settles in, his bodily confinement is compounded by resistance to a mental accommodation of his predicament. Engaged in increasingly dehumanizing and humiliating subject—object interactions, his "narrativized space" becomes an almost serial haptic farce as, time after time, his body fails to accommodate comfortably to technologies, objects and interpersonal encounters within Tokyo's built environment. The Suntory photo shoot requires inane and stereotypical movie-star poses. He is directed to project the intensity of a Frank Sinatra gaze as he becomes increasingly commoditized as an anachronistic Hollywood caricature.

His stilted posturing befits his oversized suit, cinched together to fit. A torrent of instruction in Japanese by an arrogant director is perceived as a verbal assault. The brief translation supplied by the director's assistant prompts Bob to ask if there is more to it. Something is lost in the translation. From the perspective of the viewer, Bob's "lived space" becomes our own, as we experience the sequential siege with him. The film "maps tangible sites" as its "perceived, conceived and lived space ... embody the viewer" (Bruno 1997, p. 20).

The film's primary venue, an upscale Tokyo hotel, binds the newly-wed Charlotte, a recent Harvard graduate, to Bob's transient, awkward existence. Neglected by her young, ambitious photographer husband, she is along for the ride. The architectural production of space, which constitutes the film's *mise en scène*, provides a "habitus" for the encounter and bonding of individuals who might otherwise not have crossed paths (Shapiro 2007). As is well known, since the age of merchandizing and the production of consumer desire, architecture's spatial effects have facilitated not only consuming dynamics but also the classification and collective bonding of consumers. William Leach, who chronicles the rise of American consumerism during the 1890-1930 period, puts it this way:

> along with the enhancement of goods through decoration and display and the reliance on such devices as glass cases, mirrors, elevators, and escalators, merchants endowed interiors with social meaning, some of it meant to reflect middle-class tastes, some to meet working-class needs, and whatever was left over to address both "class" and "mass" together. (Leach 1993, p. 78)

Though Bob and Charlotte appear to share upper-middle-class backgrounds, providing them access to an upscale hotel, their marked age difference, in the absence of any associative connections, would otherwise make extended close proximal habitation unlikely.

Charlotte tentatively explores the hotel's immediate confines during her husband's lengthy absences and in the process crosses paths with Bob in the hotel elevator. Subsequent encounters at the hotel bar and pool become the venues of their shared and developing Tokyo biographies. Idle views of the cityscape and television screens hasten their seeking of refuge in one another's company. The hotel's dimly lit interior, reflective surfaces and upmarket furnishings provide a sensual backdrop for their association.

Leach (1993, p. 72) describes such production of seductive exterior/interior spaces as "theatrical strategies", whose manipulations of decor and origins of enticement commenced with the onset of twentieth-century innovations and American consumer culture. Strategies of mood and emotion were used by emerging American corporate businesses to elicit and satisfy consumer demands, such as preoccupations with "comfort and bodily well-being, with luxury, spending, and acquisition" (Leach 1993, p. xiii).

Although their initial relationship is problematic, Bob and Charlotte's interactions become increasingly erotic; an eroticism that never crosses the threshold of sexual impulse and desire. The film depicts these interactions within haptic space as corporeal, tender exchanges; a sensuality that is mitigated by the physical architecture. The potential sexual relationship acts as a subtext, which is superimposed by the architectural habitus within which it transpires. Their relationship proceeds from the hotel to karaoke and strip clubs, bars and restaurants, which present alternate "spaces of consumption and consumption of space" (Bruno 1997, p. 20); as Bruno aptly states, the cinematic process in which "providing space for living and lodging sites of biography, film and architecture are constantly reinvented as stories of the flesh" (p. 21).

In a parallel architectural narrative within the film, we witness panoramas of Tokyo's vast avenues of neon-lit building facades, digital projections on towering screens, and multi-tiered levels of train, automobile, commercial and commuter traffic, which showcase a city in continual transit and motion. We see subway route maps at Shibuya, bullet trains to Kyoto and tourists in alley noodle shops exhibiting the "architectural habitus" as "building 'sets' of dwelling in motion" (Bruno 1997, p. 20). The two narratives are integrated through the film's articulation of haptic space. We are able to observe Tokyo as a space that articulates an economy of embodiment, of spatial orientation of self to other, and provides sites of tangibility, by which cinema and architecture open mobile paths that create the conditions of possibility for encounter and exploration.

Following initial farewells, *en route* to the airport, Bob sees Charlotte on the city streets. In the film's last sequence, he backtracks and embraces her with an inaudible whisper amidst the bustle of pedestrian traffic. It is the film's last evocation of a fraught haptic space, which Bruno notes is "the space of one's lived experiences ... inhabited sites narrativized by motion" — space as the shared dimension of living in film and the city, which Italians term *vissuto* (Bruno 1997, p. 20).

In order to underscore the application of Bruno's analytic of haptic space, we can note the way that Tokyo as an architectural habitus shapes Bob's individuated body—space experiences. Bob expresses his individuality in a continual performance of corporeal—spatial articulation. He extracts an individuality in resistance to the pressures of a paradoxical urban alienation; a juxtaposition of crowded interpersonal spaces and demands for indifference, which both define and negate individuality. Bob's physical and social inhibitions within Tokyo's city life articulate his embodied defense mechanisms in response to a perceived siege of stimuli. His initial inability to accommodate Tokyo's homogenizing pressures and confusing cultural codes is expressed by his bumbling physicality. However, if we heed a cinematic narrative that foregrounds Bob's bodily comportment, we witness a developing awareness of individuation, for example, in Bob's alternating aloof reserve and comical demeanor in social interactions. His body signals an effective reclamation of the spatial habitus as his antics change it from an inhibiting milieu to a place of individuated agency. The change in Bob's bodily comportment is exemplified in one of the film's comic sequences — his negotiation of hospital admission procedure, his subsequent wheelchair antics, his bodily postures in the waiting area, and his conversant miming with an elderly Japanese woman.

Bob's frequently blasé and exaggerated physiognomy signifies his ambivalent response to urban values, goods and services as a perceived siege on his sensibilities. As Georg Simmel (1903, p. 19) notes, in the metropolis "extremities and peculiarities and individualizations must be produced and they must be over-exaggerated merely to be brought into the awareness of the individual himself" (see Figure 1).

From one angle, life is made infinitely more easy in the sense that stimulations, interests and the taking up of time and attention present themselves from all sides and carry it in a stream which scarcely requires any individual efforts for its ongoing. But from another angle, life is composed more and more of these impersonal cultural elements and existing goods and values which seek to suppress peculiar personal interests and incomparabilities. (Simmel 1903, p. 19)

Among other things, Bob's experience of Tokyo has special resonance when one recognizes its difference from typical images of the US city. Tokyo's *"vernacular architecture"* (Hayden 1997, p. 85), its production of space, its shaping and inhabitation by urban residents, presents an alternate spatial dialectic to American global city counterparts as varied as New York or Los Angeles. Specifically, Tokyo's ontological urban context reveals a homology discerned primarily by regionally ethnic, social and economic class distinctions and their vernacular articulation. Tokyo, as Richard Lloyd Parry points out, is

> a "city of tribes", each with its own gathering place — Shibuya, where Japanese schoolgirls loll in their extravagant make-up, tiny skirts and monstrous platform

Figure 1 Bob's physiognomy and response.

boots; Shinjuku, where gangsters, pimps and bar girls lurk beneath a *Bladerunner* landscape of skyscrapers and noodle bars; and Akihabara where computer and electronics enthusiasts gather to buy the latest gadgets. (Lloyd Parry 2000)

It is instructive here to contrast Los Angeles neighborhoods, in which the ethnoscape exhibits a spatially produced and juxtaposed immigrant ethnic heterogeneity. In Hayden's (1997, p. 85) terms, Los Angeles displays a *"vernacular architecture"* which "changes almost as fast as costume, menus or slang". She further defines the imagery:

> An Anglo supermarket becomes a Korean American Christian church, with a billboard advertising grace instead of cantaloupes. An African American home for young working women becomes a shelter for homeless Central American refugees. An Anglo American apartment complex in San Fernando Valley is taken over by one thousand Cambodian residents, who organize it as if it were a traditional village. (Hayden 1997, p. 85)

Common building styles, spatio-temporally specific within cityscapes, reflect unique historical, social and cultural cartographies. Accordingly, noting Los Angeles' exemplary spatial and cultural context, Hayden writes:

> These overlapping groups produce an energetic, chaotic street scene, full of surprises. Jewish restaurants offer kosher burritos; a restaurant in Little Tokyo displays a plastic pizza in the front window as if it were sushi. In this context, concepts like "high culture," "ethnic purity," "cultural identity," "beauty," and "fine arts" are absurdities and anachronisms. Like it or not, we are attending the funeral of modernity and the birth of a new culture. (Hayden 1997, p. 85)

If Tokyo's inhabitants are categorized as a generally homogenous culture, then this ascription comprises foreigner and non-foreigner classifications. Homogeneity dominates in many architectural contexts, as in the subway, for example. Nevertheless, each district has its distinct heterogeneous articulation of Japan's urban culture. Uguisudani, located in an older part of Tokyo, is still configured with narrow streets of old wooden buildings; homes that survived the American firebombing of Tokyo in World War II. It still retains some of the traditional plebeian features of old Edo, such as *shitamachi* ("towns below" — those beneath the castle yet still within city limits).[1] In contrast, the hills became the westernized Yamanote, occupying most of Tokyo.[2]

Presently, Roppongi is an area where the highest concentration of foreigners can be seen; Tokyo's equivalent of "sin city". Prostitutes from the former Soviet Republics line the neon-lit avenues and facades. Korean, Chinese and Japanese offer *massagi*. Hard Rock Café and Wolfgang Puck restaurants front the streets, next to the widely proliferated fast-food chains, more traditional noodle shops and 24-hour video game rooms.

---

1. See 'Tokyo: Uguisudani', http://www.links.net/vita/trip/japan/tokyo/uguisudani/
2. See 'Tokyo: Shitamachi', http://www.links.net/vita/trip/japan/tokyo/shitamachi/

International visitors flock to this district, as well as "legions of army men on R & R, [and] software engineers in town for a few days".[3] Two male tourists tell of an effective response they used to a Nigerian man pitching the sex trade. Stating that "I'm not interested" invited further haggling; the recommended reply preventing additional rebuttal is: "Excuse me, we are good Christian gentlemen".

González Iñárritu's Tokyo

In the film *Babel* (2006), Alejandro González Iñárritu provides additional insights into Tokyo's diversity and the effect of its absorption into the info-structural age. Digital space in the form of a two-way video mobile phone incorporates technology as an extension of Chieko (Rinko Kikuchi), the hearing- and speech-impaired Japanese teenager. As she communicates in sign language across screens with her friend, her human connection through the device may be perceived as less alienating; it is an interrelation more specifically directed towards her person than the sealed preclusion of sound and rhythm in the outside world.

This aspect of *Babel*'s Tokyo can be made intelligible by resort to Ernst Bloch's micro-phenomenologies. Bloch (1972, p. 48) postulates that technology and ideology as socio-economic phenomena are each a function of the other. He elaborates that the consumption of technology is inseparable from its relevant social context. It is evident that this theoretical exposition by Bloch pre-dates the "digital revolution". He was primarily concerned with technology as an agent of production; with how products and the mechanical modes of their assembly engendered socio-economic class distinctions within an industrial era. Technology continues to contextualize human ontology. Mapping Bloch's insights onto *Babel*'s film sequences, we as viewers experience Chieko's immersion in moving crowds, surrounded by pulsations of light and other kinesthetic effects that disturb the body's orientation to space. González Iñárritu digitally reconstructs Chieko's experience of Tokyo's sensorium as our own (see Figure 2). As she makes her way through Tokyo's recreational spaces, the viewer simultaneously experiences the same dialogical digitality of Tokyo's "lived space" (Bruno 1997, p. 20). As González Iñárritu silences sound and rhythm, we become as bewildered as Chieko, installed in digital screens of images and light intra-cinematically to backdrops in a discotheque. The "lived space" of Chieko and the viewer becomes mobilized in trajectories of digital production. The ontological relevance is such that, as Peter Sands (2003, p. 129) states, "the drive toward highly connective computer technologies alters the long standing relationship between place and production". Place and production become technologized in digital information within venues of financial communication and entertainment production. Technologized space is also represented in *Lost in Translation* in the form of digital projections on colossal screens towering above the street on building facades as well as in hotel mechanization and automatons.

---

3. All quotes in this paragraph are from 'Tokyo: Roppongi', http://www.links.net/vita/trip/japan/tokyo/roppongi/

Figure 2 Chieko's (Rinko Kikuchi) experience of Tokyo's sensorium.

Cultural Practices: Appropriations of Aesthetic Space and Sensibilities

The filmic reflection of Tokyo's urban life in *Lost in Translation* and *Babel*'s Tokyo sequences is replete with images of adapted Western popular culture and "kitsch" in its variant forms. The karaoke performances in *Lost in Translation*, as gesticulated, content-exaggerated sentimentality of Western pop songs, and televised caricatures of American celebrities are some examples. *Babel* depicts teenage hang-outs, fast-food venues, dance clubs, urban recreational spaces and fashionable attire as economic and cultural appropriations of the occidental aesthetic of urban space and architecture. Ben Highmore (2005, p. 14) describes the Japanese adaptation of Western influences, the "cross-cultural pollination" of East and West, as an adaptation of "new regimes of visual language to specific cultural ends ... outside cultural practices are adapted and refashioned in particular local contexts". It emphasizes the influence of Japanese "visual production" and the Western appropriation of the Eastern aesthetic in architecture and art. He cites "internationalism" and "creative cosmopolitanism" as a "driving force for modernity" in the urban: "Architects who laid out blueprints for the modern city, architects who fashioned the modular block-like structures that fill our cities, did so by looking at Japanese building, adopting and adapting their aesthetic strategies ... and practices" (ibid.). The following examination of genres provides further insight into the cultural appropriations of the urban aesthetic.

Artistic Practice and Animation

Highmore's evocation of the historical influence of Japanese art in international exhibitions of the 1860s and '70s helps us recognize what is observed if we pay attention to the prints of Japanese woodcut artists. Woodcut prints by Ando Hiroshige and Katsushika Hokusai were reinterpreted in the artwork of Monet, Degas, van Gogh and others. *Manga*, a book of Hokusai's woodblock prints, "became an essential ingredient for the so-called French impressionists ... such as Toulouse-Lautrec, ... to register the intensity of Parisian urban modernity" (Highmore 2005, p. 14). Manga and anime (caricature in comic books or animation which is reminiscent of the Japanese graphics of nineteenth-century woodblock artists), an aesthetic form of expression, as a genre is a reappropriation of Japanese art via Western influence of cartoonist design, yet adapted in a unique Japanese visual medium of communication.

One such example of a Japanese adaptation of visual communication is *Akira*, a comic book series which is of greater volume than its American counterpart. Originating as manga, it has also been adapted in animated form. The *Akira* series deals "with motorcycle gangs in Neo-Tokyo many years after an atomic devastation" (Carey 2004, p. 6). Akira is the name of "an immense, malevolent apocalyptic device or person, both actually, that still lay dormant at the center of the city" (ibid.). Its storylines depict worlds past and present, inspired by interpretations of historical disaster events and apocalyptic visions of urban annihilation. Peter Carey (ibid.) comments that "on Akira's graphic pages I found images so artful that I could imagine hanging them on my wall".

Anime, as another visual medium in Japan, is "not limited to a specific age group and ... is respected as a live action film". Its French word adaptation is perhaps due to the woodblock influence of French art (Carey 2004, p. 6). Often illustrating personal stories of tragedy, *The Grave of the Fireflies* by the director Isao Takahata is such an anime film, dramatizing the novel of the same name. Both genres depict the American firebombing of the Shitamachi and Yamanote districts of Tokyo in 1944. The anime depicts a tragic narrative about a teenage boy Seita and his younger sister Setsuko. Their mother killed, their father serving in the navy and rejected by their aunt, they abandon the burning world of Tokyo and attempt to survive in the mountains. Unable to feed his sister, who dies of malnutrition, Seita returns to the destruction in Tokyo and dies in a railway station (Carey 2004, p. 75).

Architecture

The cultural and economic appropriation of traditional and modern "spaces", as in the architecture within the expressive texts of these genres, is in Tokyo, as in the case of other "global cities", seemingly infinite. Traditional cultural "spatial" practices as expressive variant forms are embodied appropriations within the aesthetic modalities of the urban and the rural. Linda Krause and Patrice Petro (2003, p. 2) speak of "meaningful communication"; the contextualization of "global cities" from interdisciplinary perspectives "spanning architectural theory and practice, film studies, sociology, literature, cultural studies, rhetoric and political science". The seeming dichotomy as juxtapositions of traditional and urban modern structure within or outside Tokyo's city limits may be a false determination, due to the interwoven genre contexts of practiced cultural appropriations of aesthetic space and sensibilities. As exemplified previously, manga and anime are not only aesthetic mediums of cross-cultural influences, but also expressions of capitalist modernity's imprint on more traditional Japanese artistic form.

In the market space of the urban city and rural landscape, the two-valued orientation of modern versus traditional modalities of practice may be presented as such, perhaps as exploited visuals or iconographies for consumer-accessible spatial production. Tourist attractions in Kyoto encompass the taking of photographs with geisha girls in traditional attire and make-up, the patronage of gift shops selling numerous souvenir replicas of Buddha, and calendar pictorials of traditional Japanese weddings and pristine temple gardens. In a city which is in many ways the epitome of the modern, spaces created by modern technology compete with others that are more traditional. For example, Tokyo's cityscape incorporates various forms of traditional aesthetic cultural practice and expression: the *kabuki* theater, the temple of Senso-ji, the Meji Shrine and the museums of Ueno Park (Lloyd Parry 2000). Within the urban streetscape are numerous microcosms; facsimiles of traditional aesthetic space such as venues of "authentic Japanese cuisine", clothing, ritual and worship, gardens and natural environments.

"The Lost Arts"

Modern Tokyo is somehow effacing Japan's traditional cultural practices and aesthetic forms. It is a lament heard between the layers of historical context; between ritual and modern practice. For example, the traditional artistic renderings on *byobu* ("paneled wall screens") and *kakejiko* ("hanging scrolls") have given way to the "disneyfication" of visual language. The lament continues from the diminished practice of the horticultural art and aesthetic of *ikebana* ("flower arranging") and *bonsai* ("cultivation of 'dwarf' trees") to the replacement of traditional musical instruments with a techno beat. The lament itself transforms into a song, as a mournful deliberation of aesthetic sensibilities, diverse as the vocals of practitioners of cultural forms. Nostalgia for "the lost arts" is a universal theme within "global cities". Tokyo may be unique here only in its interpretation of loss.

However such loss may be perceived by inhabitants in continual flux, the gradual disappearance of traditional cultural practice is not as absolute as its existence in its purest form. The dynamics of changing social contexts, if ever so slightly or dramatically, affect how traditional cultural practices are reconstituted and reappropriated within the shifting contexts of the urban modern and postmodern aesthetic. The embodiment of traditional cultural rituals as gestures, for example, in social or gender-specific protocol, is still practiced with deferential bowing or hand-shielded laughter, maintained perhaps as a social distinction within the hierarchy of urban modernity. The melding of multiform culturally-practiced appropriations of Tokyo's urban aesthetic provides potential for exponential combinations of hermeneutical exposition, expression and exploration.

The Novel

In yet another genre, the contemporary Japanese novel also participates in the cultural narrative of aesthetic appropriation. Stories of human dramas of contact and communication, of mediation, negotiation within class structure, and the social hierarchy and hegemony of Tokyo's urban life are revealed in "Shizuko Akashi" (Murakami 2004) and "A Slow Boat to China" (Murakami 1993). For example, based on real and fictitious characters, Haruki Murakami seems to focus on protagonist responses, and mental and physical composure — the embodied haptic aesthetic within journeyed space. Articulations of being, reflected in comportment of mind and body, function as mirror images and descriptive devices of protagonist spirit. Like other genres, the novel also reflects older historical events juxtaposed with the modernity of the urban aesthetic.

"Shizuko Akashi", as such a story, is a pseudonym for a girl who was mentally and physically disabled by the sarin gas attack on the Akihabara Station on the Hibiya Line of the Tokyo subway on 20 March 1995 (Murakami 2004, p. 43). Murakami interviews Shizuko, who, as a result of the gas attack, is partially paralyzed, wheelchair dependant and impaired in brain function. His observations of Shizuko detail how she copes with and relates to her environment in her disablement. He describes the humanity of their interactions:

> Something in her must be trying to break out, a precious something. But it just can't find an outlet. If only temporarily, she's lost the power and the means to enable it to come to the surface, and yet that *something* exists unharmed and intact within the walls of her inner space. When she holds someone's hand, it's all she can do to communicate that "this thing is here". (Murakami 2004, p. 51)

Shizuko's dream is going to Tokyo Disneyland. She does not recall her life prior to the attack, yet no one is quite sure if she remembers her visit there. Murakami (2004, p. 53) relates this destination in her mental register, "fixed in her mind as something like a symbol of freedom and health".

Just as we see a layering of temporality in "Shizuko Akashi", "A Slow Boat to China" narrates chronologically sequenced encounters between a Japanese resident and three Chinese residents in Tokyo. The story opens with a question: "When did I meet my first Chinese?" Murakami (1993, p. 218) depicts micro-urban worlds within these encounters: the Chinese elementary school testing site led by the Chinese proctor; the Chinese co-worker in a publisher's warehouse in Bunkyo Ward; and the high school acquaintance who strikes up a conversation of recognition and remembrance in an Aoyama Boulevard café. More than vignette descriptions of accommodation, assimilation of foreign identities, conventions and tropes, they are stories of connection to self and other. Murakami's seemingly literary emphasis on the esoteric, ephemeral particularities of the human condition engenders a specific dialectic of aesthetic sensibilities. Though he frames his stories within cultural, hegemonic contexts, the semiotics of his telling narrates a generic urban appropriation of aesthetic space and sensibilities:

> This occurs to me while I'm riding the Yamanote Line. I'm standing by the door, holding on to my ticket so I won't lose it, gazing out the window at the buildings as we pass. Our city, these streets, I don't know why it makes me so depressed. That old familiar gloom that befalls the city dweller, regular as due dates, cloudy as mental Jell-O. The dirty facades, the nameless crowds, the unremitting noise, the packed rush-hour trains, the gray skies, the billboards on every square centimeter of available space, the hopes and resignation, irritation and excitement. And everywhere, infinite options, infinite possibilities. An infinity, and at the same time zero. That's the city. (Murakami 1993, p. 238)

Cinema

In Charles Baudelaire's (poetic) rendering of the urban and its dweller, those who walk the streets — "wandering subversives" — are detached from mainstream bourgeois society. Conversely, if we turn to Walter Benjamin (1968, pp. 172-173), he, unlike Baudelaire, did not view the *flâneur* as an aimless wanderer, although a separate "man of the crowd", but rather as one who is self-assertive. He is detached; he is one who would not allow himself "to be jostled by the crowd"; he is itinerant, neither always leisurely nor entangled in "the feverish turmoil of the city" (ibid.).

Returning to the filmic Tokyo traversed by Bob and Charlotte in *Lost in Translation*, both Baudelaire's *flâneur* analytic and Benjamin's subsequent reinterpretation can be applied through Giuliana Bruno's insights. The transient and chance encounters of Bob and Charlotte's urban experience become compounded by their visitor status. Both Bob and Charlotte are business travelers: he for a photo shoot and she by way of her photographer husband, who is also involved in marketing. The production and sale of images bound to Tokyo's marketplace link Bob and Charlotte in their experiential movement from what Giuliana Bruno refers to as "optic to haptic". Beyond recreational, sight-oriented travel, Bob and Charlotte experience Tokyo's architecture within a specified cartography. The hotel is seemingly selected by Bob's employer as he is met by Japanese business associates in the lobby; a selection process is also implied in the case of Charlotte's career-driven husband. The film's "spatio-corporeal kinetics" transforms Bob and Charlotte, like the viewer, from spectators as *voyeurs* to *voyageurs*. Bruno's erroneous spelling of "sight-seeing" as "site-seeing" inter- and intra-cinematically signals the shift from movement by sight to movement by embodiment (Bruno 1997, p. 10).

The *voyageur/voyageuse* in Giuliana Bruno's analysis lends a partial understanding to the definition of the *flâneur/flâneuse* in Charles Baudelaire's and Walter Benjamin's analytics. Both articulate a spatio-corporeal definition of the itinerant. Baudelaire departs from his earlier social classifications (for example, artist, prostitute) of the urban wanderer, or the definition of *flâneur* by criteria of authority ("Mythologies of Modernity"). Rather, the urban itinerant is, in Baudelaire's conceptualization, physiologically and psychologically detached from participation in mainstream society. Benjamin's reinterpretation of the *flâneur* as detached, yet physically assertive within the urban crowd, characterizes the itinerant's embodied articulation as purposeful and leisurely. As an urban wanderer, Bob's detachment from his surroundings is expressed by his bodily comportment, stiff and reserved in a crowded elevator, his head towering above the rest, or lackadaisical in a hospital waiting room. Situation and site map his physical responses. His resistance to subordinating himself to the pronounced social hierarchy and conventions within Tokyo's urban mass reflects his refusal, as Walter Benjamin states, "to be jostled by the crowd". The ambiguity of his authority as an American actor, catered to by business associates yet humiliated by an arrogant Japanese director, illuminates a paradox within Tokyo's urban hierarchy. His authority from having "guest status" is alternately marginalized by being considered an "outsider".

Turning to Benjamin and Baudelaire and their characterization of the urban crowd, the spatio-corporeal analytic re-emerges. Benjamin, in *Charles Baudelaire*, characterized his assessment of *Verfassung* ("physiognomy", "comportment") and the motivational purpose of urban crowds as unrealistic (Benjamin 1974, p. 35). Baudelaire perceived this crowd as chaotic in hypersensitivity to the stimuli of the city environment. He characterized the city person as feeling inadequate and fatigued, suffering psychosomatically and as a consumer prone to the "evils" of commercial culture. The urban "mass" in Benjamin's assessment bears greater composure and order, provoking less fear as a collective in absorbed, fascinated transit (Benjamin 1974, p. 36).

In applying these characterizations, we recall Chieko from *Babel*'s Tokyo sequence. Her hearing impairment intensifies her perceptual responses to stimuli within Tokyo's urban mass. The film's director, Alejandro González Iñárritu, seems to focus on her sense of isolation, as a teenager struggling with social acceptance, unmet needs of affection and recognition of her humanity. He does so in montage sequences that reflect the urban analytic of Benjamin and Baudelaire. The discotheque sequence comes to life in the manic movement of the dance crowd, the rapid beams of lights and vibrations of beat. Chieko becomes bewildered by the loss of her dance partner to her friend; she is stunned by the additional physical isolation to her hearing impairment. She flees the disco crowd, overwhelmed by the chaos. Her subsequent detached purview of the scene evokes an analysis of the superficiality and Baudelaire-referenced "evils" of commercial culture.

Iñárritu's montage cut to Chieko on the city sidewalk highlights her isolation; as indifferent to the pedestrian crowd as they are to her in absorbed transit. The bumping of a passer-by elicits no response from Chieko. Thus, consistent with Benjamin's assessment, Tokyo's pedestrian crowd bears an ordered composure, an almost autopiloted traversal. The indifference of the city dweller may be alternately defined by Baudelaire as characteristic of fatigue and psychosomatic suffering. Chieko's father embodies this characterization in the long working hours of Tokyo's inhabitants. Iñárritu seems to cast this as an embodiment of dysfunction within urban life. As a surviving single parent, Chieko's father is unable to address many of her needs. He returns to their apartment later in the evening, in time to avert Chieko's potential re-enactment of her mother's suicide.

Conclusion

The utilization of cinema's narrational space becomes pertinent in the examination of spatial/temporal appropriations of architecture. The modality of cinematic technology and its production of "being space" — haptic space as it relates body to structure — is reinhabited as the camera lens captures moments missed by the protagonist and film viewer alike. Cinematic technique such as montage reassembles lived experiences non-chronologically, much as non-sequential memory informs the knowledge of our "being" in the present. Moving out of the "theories of the eye", the "spatio-corporeal kinetics" of cinema provides a modern ontological cartography (Bruno 1997, p. 10). Spectatorship as inter- and intra-cinematic sightseeing gives way to "site-seeing" by film's "mobile map" (Bruno 1997, p. 9).

The site of cinema becomes an actor in the positioning of the body's self to other. It positions its object and practice on the body through its own dynamic. It is the positioning of the body in relation to space that informs individual collective practices of lived experiences and identity construction. Observing the filmic characters Bob and Chieko, we see people whose city experiences trump their territorial identities. What looms larger are their positionings within Tokyo's urban life world.

Ultimately, Sofia Coppola's film title *Lost in Translation* provides a relevant reference inasmuch as it reframes the critical inquiry of political life within Tokyo's urban environment. In addition, a consideration of varied genres reinforces Coppola's cinematic insights. Through cinema, art, animation, architecture and the novel, one can investigate political life within the urban sensorium.

Ryokan serene
Akiko-san she so loves
Hinamatsuri[4]

---

4. "Hinamatsuri", also seen spelled as "Hina Matsuri", is Japanese for the Japanese Girl's Day celebration.

References

Babel (2006) dir. Alejandro González Iñárritu, Paramount Pictures, USA.
Benjamin, W. (1968) *Illuminations*, trans. Zohn, H., Schocken Books, New York.
Benjamin, W. (1974) *Charles Baudelaire*, Suhrkamp, Frankfurt.
Bloch, E. (1972) *Vom Hasard zur Katastrophe: Politische Aufsätze aus den Jahren 1934-1939*, Suhrkamp, Frankfurt.
Bruno, G. (1997) 'Site-seeing: Architecture and the Moving Image', *Wide Angle*, vol. 19, no. 4, pp. 8-24.
Carey, P. (2004) *Wrong about Japan*, Vintage Books, New York.
Eisenstein, S. M. (1989) 'Montage and Architecture', with an introduction by Y.-A. Bois, trans. Glenny, M., *Assemblage*, no. 10, pp. 110-131.
Hayden, D. (1997) *The Power of Place: Urban Landscapes as Public History*, MIT Press, Cambridge, MA.
Highmore, B. (2005) *Cityscapes: Cultural Readings in the Material and Symbolic City*, Palgrave Macmillan, New York.
Krause, L. & Petro, P. (2003) 'Introduction', in Krause, L. & Petro, P. (eds), *Global Cities: Cinema, Architecture, and Urbanism in a Digital Age*, Rutgers University Press, New Brunswick, NJ.
Leach, W. (1993) *Land of Desire: Merchants, Power, and the Rise of a New American Culture*, Vintage Books, New York.
Lloyd Parry, R. (2000) 'Tokyo: The City That's Stranger Than Fiction', *The Independent*, 25 June, http://travel.independent.co.uk/asia/article166708.ece.
Lost in Translation (2003) dir. Sofia Coppola, Universal Studios, USA.
Murakami, H. (1993) 'A Slow Boat to China', in *The Elephant Vanishes*, Vintage Books, New York.
Murakami, H. (2004) 'Shizuko Akashi', in *Vintage Murakami*, Vintage Books, New York.
'Mythologies of Modernity', http://fds.oup.com/www.oup.co.uk/pdf/0-19-818682-7.pdf.
Sands, P. (2003) 'Global Cannibal City Machines: Recent Visions of Urban/Social Space', in Krause, L. & Petro, P. (eds), *Global Cities: Cinema, Architecture, and Urbanism in a Digital Age*, Rutgers University Press, New Brunswick, NJ.
Shapiro, M. J. (2007) 'Research Methods Political Science 702', Lecture, University of Hawaii at Manoa, Honolulu, HI, 26 February.
Simmel, G. (1903) 'Chapter 1: The Metropolis and Mental Life', http://www.blackwell-publishing. com/content/BPL_Images/Conent_store/Sample_chapter/063 225137/ Bridge. pdf.

Policing Paris[1]: Private Publics and Architectural Media in Michael Haneke's *Caché*

Brianne Gallagher

Locating Paris as a central site to explore national anxieties surrounding the immigrant subject in France, this article turns to Michael Haneke's 2005 film *Caché* (*Hidden*), which offers an important counter-narrative of the state's desire to depoliticize the continuation of colonial practices in the present. While the private space of the home and the public space of the media are often seen as opposing spheres in dominant imaginaries, Haneke collapses these distinctions by highlighting colonialism's present violences through the multiple home spaces of Paris. Turning to various home spaces in the film allows the viewer to enter the more hidden territorializations of colonial violence often relegated as "private" matters within nation-state narratives of a coherent national "public" culture. Moreover, by politicizing more dominant political boundaries/borders between public and private space in the home itself, the film offers a radical critique of the privation of privacy and modern architecture as media. This move, the author suggests finally, provides an additional critique of the ways in which national ideas of the French "family", "security", and immigrant "other" are highly policed categories of knowledge enacted in part through the individual.

Introduction

Massive immigration has only just begun. It is the biggest problem facing France, Europe and probably the world. We risk being submerged. (Jean-Marie Le Pen, BBC News 2002)

If we do not develop ... Africa ... if we do not make available the necessary resources to bring about this development, these people will flood the world. (Jacques Chirac, BBC News 2006)

---

1. I use the term 'policing' here in a Deleuzian sensibility that underlines the shift from the disciplinary societies of the eighteenth and nineteenth centuries, which Foucault outlined, to what Deleuze calls 'mechanisms of control' operating in current 'societies of control'. Whereas disciplinary societies were organized around spaces of enclosure, such as the factory, societies of control are organized on a more mobile grid of global networks, such as the global corporation. For a more detailed discussion on societies of control, see Deleuze (1992).

A "society [that] must be defended" emerges in these two statements by Le Pen and Chirac, or, more to the point, a Western society/world bound by its difference to an ever-impeding threat: total annihilation by the immigrant other.[2] The widely publicized national anxieties surrounding the movement of peoples across France's borders, along with the state's attempts to grapple with its resulting changing ethnoscape and its related colonial "past", recalls Mathieu Kassovitz's 1995 film *La Haine* (*Hate*), which locates Paris as a site where racial tensions surrounding the immigrant play out in the multiple spaces of the city's *banlieues*. In *La Haine*, Paris is more a geopolitical space of racial class tensions than a city of light; a space where violent encounters between immigrant groups in the city's *banlieues* structure everyday life and their multiple imaginings of the past, present and future. While each character in *La Haine* envisions different futures and alternative understandings of the present, each character is also confronted daily with police surveillance and violence, subject to spectacularization by the media, and positioned as an individual threat to the state. In Foucault's terms, each immigrant subject is narrated by the state's apparatus of "security" as a socio-political-biological threat capable of "infiltrating the social body" and thus in need of control, containment and representation (Foucault 2003, p. 61).

While both the immigrants moving across France's borders and those living in the *banlieues* are totalized in national narratives as biopolitical threats, who else is in need of control, containment and representation in Le Pen and Chirac's calls to arms? State apparatuses of policing operate not only by identifying threats but also by affirming ideas of a coherent, though multiple, "diverse" French society as the target of the threat. A society to be defended must ask itself what it means to be a French "people"; what aspects of collective identity remain to be defended; whether there is anything remaining that can be identified as distinctive French culture. Chirac's call for "development" of Africa as a necessary solution to thwart the risk of a "flood" of African people is an instance of the state's attempt to excite public imaginaries of what it means to be a unified national society against a dangerous other. His call, more recently, to affirm a "Europe of culture" (Chirac 2005) illustrates the state's attempt to keep the driving force of a unitary French nationhood of different but common equals alive. Doubtless, juridical measures directed toward "solving" the "problem" of immigration are not enough. The state's solution to immigration depends, increasingly, on the *society's* self-reflection on what it means to be a French citizen, on what constitutes good French character, and on how policy can be formulated to encourage immigrants to seek the same dreams all French citizens seek: family, citizenship, and economic and social prosperity through hard work (as the "virtues" tend to be expressed in official discourse).

These state "solutions" thus involve imposing a broad social consensus on what constitutes Frenchness and an insistence that immigrants shed their otherness.

---

2. The quoted expression is the title of Michel Foucault's 1975-1976 lectures at the Collège de France (see Foucault 2003). The title is apropos of the contemporary anti-immigration situation in France, for Foucault notes that at a particular historical point, the concept of 'raced struggle' turned into racism.

In short, the approach seeks to depoliticize difference by attempting to erase it. In response to such a perspective, Jacques Rancière writes:

> Depoliticizing conflicts in order to settle them, or stripping otherness of any yardstick the better to solve its problems — this is the madness which our time identifies with a reasonable and easy democracy that harmonizes state initiatives with the natural tendencies of productive society, with its efforts and desires. (Rancière 1995, p. 106)

Rancière calls our attention to the ways in which politics (as a form of policy) involves a consensus on whom and what is deemed sensible, understandable, visible and audible in the distribution of the sensible (see Rancière 2004). Consensus, he writes, is the "loss of any measure of otherness" (Rancière 1995, p. 104) wherein "[t]he folly of our times is the wish to use consensus to cure the diseases of consensus" (p. 106). This is why disagreement and organized dissent are crucial for Rancière in restoring the "political" to politics. Politics, he writes, "revolves around what is seen and what can be said about it, around who has the ability to see and the talent to speak, around the properties of spaces and the possibilities of time" (Rancière 1995, p. 13). In the moment that disagreement restores visibility to the subject once invisible and repartitions the sensible, there will again remain an excess of difference that still falls outside the new redivision. Following Rancière and *La Haine*'s challenge to approach Paris as a contested space of political legitimacy, I turn to Michael Haneke's film *Caché* (*Hidden*), which offers a subtle but important counter-narrative to the state's attempt to dissolve disagreement amongst the "nation" on the "problem" of immigration and colonialist histories in present-day Paris.

Repartitioning Private Matters

Michael Haneke's suspense-thriller *Caché* (2005) follows the deterioration of French television talk-show host Georges Laurent (Daniel Auteuil) and his wife Anne's (Juliette Binoche) family harmony. In the opening shot sequences, the camera centers on the outside of the Laurents' home for several prolonged minutes, until, unexpectedly, the footage of the home rewinds before the viewer on the screen. In the following shot, the viewer enters the Laurents' home where Anne and Georges watch the footage of their home (the same home footage from the previous shot) on their television screen. At this point, the viewer learns that the couple has received surveillance footage of their home from an anonymous sender, left in a plastic bag on their porch. At first, Anne and Georges suspect that the surveillance footage of their home might be a "schoolboy" prank, perhaps from one of their son's friends at school. However, the Laurents become increasingly frantic as additional surveillance tapes of their home, including violent childlike drawings of a young boy covered in blood, are delivered to their doorstep, workplaces, and to their son's school by the anonymous sender over the next few days. Like the photograph's function in Wang and Auster's film

Smoke (1995), where a colossal collection of Auggie's snapshots of daily city life on a New York street corner propels a reluctant Paul to remember a hidden, painful past on spotting a photograph of his deceased wife in Auggie's album, drawings and surveillance footage in *Caché* operate to position the violence of the past as a necessary condition of the present. Georges presumes the sender of the violent drawings to be Majid (Maurice Bénichou); an orphan son of an Algerian family that Georges's family adopted when he was a child.

In several dazzling flashback sequences, the viewer learns that Georges resented the young Majid's arrival. In the first flashback, Georges's son hands him a childlike black-and-white drawing of a boy covered in red blood that he has received in school from an anonymous sender. The camera then cuts to an exterior shot of Georges's home at night, followed by a shot that zooms in on Georges's bedroom window where a young boy sits covered in blood, looking back like one caught by a headlight into the camera at the viewer. In the second flashback, Georges visits his mother who is ill. Here we learn that Majid was sent away from Georges's upper-bourgeois family home following the Algerian War because of Georges's parents' capitulation to Georges's feelings of resentment toward the young Majid. The camera then brings us to a young Georges and Majid, standing outside the house under an open shed-like dwelling, as Georges stands with an axe while a terrified Majid presses himself against the far side of the shed's stone wall. Georges brings the axe violently down on the head of a chicken, and while it violently frolics about, he slowly approaches the terrified Majid with the axe and raises it while standing only a few steps away from him. In a cut, the viewer is brought to Georges's sudden awakening from sleep, drenched in sweat and overcome by anxiety as he lies in bed at his mother's house.

At this point in the film, it remains unclear to the viewer as to whether Georges did in fact approach Majid with an axe as a child. The viewer might assume, for instance, that the flashbacks, or possible nightmares, reflect a more symbolic imaginary of Georges's fear of Majid or resentment toward the orphan as a child. Nonetheless, because Georges is guilt-ridden and haunted by his complicity in Majid's departure (which we learn later in the film's narrative), he remains convinced that the anonymous sender of the packages is, indeed, Majid. Giving into this (unwarranted) assumption, he visits Majid in his rundown apartment on several occasions. Although Majid denies any connection to the drawings and surveillance footage, Georges insists that Majid must be the culprit, doubtless because he evokes Georges's psychic culprit, himself. But Majid also evokes a national-level guilt. For Georges, Majid is the culprit because of his deep resentment toward Georges's upper-class privilege and career success as a public media figure, and because of his forced departure from the family home as a child. For France, Majid evokes the colonial culprit — French colonial policy.

Several scenes later, Georges returns home to find Anne watching a videotape of Georges and Majid's encounter in Majid's apartment taped by an anonymous viewer. It is important to note that at this point in the film the viewer, Anne, and family friends are unaware that Georges has visited Majid at his apartment. Neither does the viewer know who Majid is and why he was forced to leave the home as a child. After watching the encounter between Majid and Georges on video, Anne, frustrated with her husband's silence, presses Georges for an explanation. A reluctant Georges confesses to Anne that his parents planned to adopt the young boy after Majid's parents, who worked for the Laurents, were killed during the 1961 peaceful mass pro-FLN (National Liberation Front) demonstrations in Paris, when the Paris police drowned over 200 Algerian protestors in the Seine. Georges resented both Majid for intruding on the family space of the home and his parents' desire to adopt him: "My parents decided to adopt the boy. I don't know why. They felt responsible in some way." Recalling the flashback sequences and violent drawings, the viewer can suspect at this point that Georges lied to his parents about Majid cutting off the head of a chicken, and perhaps even a violent fight between the two boys, in order to force Majid to leave the home. Later in the film, in a disturbing scene, Majid calls Georges's to visit his apartment. Entering Majid's kitchen, Majid turns to Georges and says, "I wanted you to be present". At this point Majid then slits his own throat. In this colonial allegory, the effacement of the more hidden colonial violences of the past (such as Majid's unnecessary departure from the family home as a child) is rendered visible as ongoing violence in the present (such as Georges's insistence that Majid is the vengeful stalker). In the end, Georges is left with his guilt-ridden angst and buries himself in his bedroom. The closing shot freeze-frames his son's school, suggesting perhaps that the future of France's colonialist guilt and violence is left to France's future generations.

However, more important to *Caché* than its narrative form are the ways in which Haneke's use of flashbacks and reverse-rewind shots disrupts linear narratives of time, and by implication, linear models of history. The reverse-rewind shots in particular disrupt the spatial composition of the cityscape and home as a free-floating image separated from politically and historically informed temporal presences. For example, in the opening shot sequence, the camera secures its gaze through an extended time shot of the home as an everyday place – a stable, quite upper-class apartment in Paris with several passers-by and soft city sounds. However, at the same time, the dominant signature of the home space as an everyday place of urban city harmony is disrupted by a digital scrolling of credits in citation-like format across the screen – a technological recording of the director's signature of the film. The director's signatory marking across the scene of the home suggests that the home is both a "natural" symbol in dominant imaginaries as well as a technologically mediated, contestable figure of authorship in media and cinema.

There is a cut from the outside of the home to its interior, allowing the viewer to enter the domestic sphere of Georges and Anne, who have received video surveillance footage of their quiet French apartment dwelling from an anonymous sender. In the next shot, the home is center-screened again. After several minutes of watching the home image, center screen, the gaze of the camera (and viewer) is interrupted as the footage of the home begins to rewind. It is at this point that the viewer discovers that the opening reel of the home is the surveillance footage left on the couple's porch. As the camera cuts to the living-room space of the Laurents' home, the viewer now watches the footage on the couple's television screen. Throughout the film, Georges and Anne turn off the footage of the home only to turn to attendant images of violence and the "war on terror" on the televisual screen, which enters the intimacy of the home. In this sense, the television screen functions as a window for seeing the home as a site of surveillance *inside* the home and as a *window* for the media.

Clearly, in *Caché*, architecture is indeed a character in the film. Crucially, the reverse-rewind shots, the camera's gaze and architectural space all mutually define each other. Like Sergei Eisenstein, Haneke's concern is with how the significance of architecture renders itself through cinematic montage. As a dynamic character, architecture frames and constitutes the objects and peoples with whom it interacts. Through montage, architecture transforms the building from "a passive setting of the action" into "a major agent of the plot" (Bois 1989, p. 113). As an agent of the plot, architectural montage in *Caché* works as a "structure of perception" and as a "decentering effect of parallax", continually resituating the spectator's gaze and reconstituting the knowledge issue by multiplying the various spatial locations of the characters and, in effect, the spectator's gaze (Bois 1989, p. 113). While Georges effects various lines of flight throughout the cityscape as he becomes a *voyageur* to public and private spaces, the architectural montage of the camera *captures* a particular knowledge of the world from the spatial loci that enframe and contain Georges, various characters and the spectator. As a result, architecture performs as a site of meaning-making. For example, the continual unknowingness as to whether the viewer is watching the characters or architectural space through the window of the cinematic camera or through an unknown other, revealed by the continual feedback loop of various scenes and their positioning within various home spaces, operates as a repetitive force in the film.

The uncertainty of the gaze acts as a repetitive, discordant rhythm, interrupting the film's dialogical narrative while impugning the idea that vision is an unproblematic, uncensored and technologically unmediated form of social control. As a result, the viewer becomes aware of his/her gaze, while the characters become aware of the gaze of the unknown "other". Haneke therefore places the "viewer in the film" at the same time that the "character has become a kind of viewer" (Deleuze 1989, p. 3), disrupting the distinction between spectator and spectacle. Giuliana Bruno's remarks about the viewing situation in film are pertinent here. She approaches cinema as a "mobile map" of "site-seeing", wherein the viewer becomes a *voyageur* rather than a mere *voyeur* in the film's "spatio-corporeal kinetics" (Bruno 1997, p. 10). Thus, while one might indeed feel like a *voyeur* in the film looking in on the various home spaces of Paris often through a series of surveillance shots, it is better to approach the film as an invitation to see the home as it is connected to multiple spaces of the city and historical forces. An attunement to the kinetics of the film yields reflection on the ways in which one experiences the city by walking around it.

Accordingly, I want to turn attention to the ways in which *Caché* maps the city by allowing the viewer to become a *voyageur*. Throughout the film, viewers move from notions of public to private space by their continual entrance into multiple home spaces. Using the home space as a central site to map Haneke's "hidden" Paris is similar to the way Walter Benjamin renders Charles Baudelaire's Paris as a Paris of "dream image[s]" (Benjamin 2006, p. 41). The home space in *Caché* is like the dream image of the prostitute in Baudelaire's city, who is the "seller and the sold in one", or the arcade that is "house no less than street" (p. 41). Indeed, it is these dream images that structure Benjamin's *The Arcades Project* (see Benjamin 2002). One can approach Benjamin's unfinished work as a precursor to Benjamin's own approach to creating a film on Paris (see Vidler 2002). Effectively, Benjamin's cinematic mapping of Paris and film form would be much like *The Arcades Project* itself: a fractured milieu of dream images and micro-narratives resisting resolution in narrative structure; a Paris, that is, of the *flâneur*, who strolls through the everyday haptic space of the arcades, streets corners, outer limits of the city and street crowds. But what, Anthony Vidler asks, might Benjamin's "plan of Paris look like?" (Vidler 2002, p. 116). How might it map the development of the city's urban structure while simultaneously "'condensing' a century of [its] history into half an hour?" (ibid.).

For Haneke, mapping the plan of Paris's urban infrastructure and history requires, specifically, mapping the domestic privacy of the home onto France's historical and *ongoing* colonial practices. The viewer is brought through various dream images of the Paris home space — through entrances and exits that oscillate between tranquil settings and often more violent ones — moving between past and present home spaces, *transmorphing* the home space into a site of contention connected to colonialist histories, erasure of individual subjects and national imperialist projects in the present. Positioning the home space in the film in relation to France's colonial historical present challenges the state's attempt to narrate colonial violences as mere remnants of the past. For example, turning to the present colonial violences in the home space of Paris challenges the museum space of the National Center of the History of Immigration which recently opened in Paris (see Kimmelman 2007). The museum is located in the affluent suburbs, far from the poorer neighborhoods in the *banlieues* where many immigrant youths rioted in 2005 in response to the growing economic and social inequalities that condition daily life for many immigrants living in France. The riots were also in response to Nicholas Sarkozy, then prime minister and now president, and his zero-tolerance anti-crime campaign targeted at immigrant populations. In contrast to the harsh realities of economic poverty and social discrimination experienced by many immigrants living in Paris, the new museum — located in a building that used to be part of the International Colonial Exposition of 1931 — narrates the history of immigration to France and the national anxieties surrounding the current immigrant population within a multicultural model of tolerance and diversity. In their essay "Landmarks — A Permanent Exhibition: 200 Years of Immigration", theater designer Pascal Payeur and museography specialist Lydia Elhadad describe the aesthetic designs they helped to implement in the museum's exhibitions. As Payeur and Elhadad describe it, the museum exhibitions are constructed around the theme of an "imaginary itinerary" which brings the museum visitor through a "shared experience" of immigration to France over the past 200 years (Payeur & Elhadad 2007, p. 73). The itinerary, they write, is "based on a play of emotions and intimacy, with actual lives of real flesh-and-blood people — beginning with their voices, the stories of immigrants and their journeys" (p. 75). This aesthetic itinerary, they further note, "creates a *coherent*, measured score, with its strong beats and it silences, which follow one another along a gallery almost 100 metres long and a dozen wide" (p. 75; my emphasis). Their description of the "leisure lounges" in the last itinerary, which represents a "multicultural France", is worth noting here:

> The leisure lounges at the end of the itinerary provide matter for reading and interpretation interactively and collectively. This is a place for sharing narratives on the diversity of mixtures and the birth of the multicultural society. Visitors can meet, share ideas and enjoy themselves around a collection of objects and music, where the very language affirms its own identity. These areas are as much about provoking questions as about entertainment. It is a pause to consider our society made up of hybrids, of mixing and sharing, and it ends this *imaginary journey* made by people who left home two centuries ago. (Payeur & Elhadad 2007, p. 77; my emphasis)

While the visitor to the National Center of the History of Immigration strolls through the "imaginary itinerary" and "imaginary journey" mapping the history of immigration in France, the viewer of *Caché* is only allowed to "see" the history of immigration in France as it is connected to past *and* present *colonial imaginaries* and colonial violences, rendered visible by Georges's movement through the multiple home spaces of Paris. As a twenty-first-century *flâneur*, Georges decodes the privileged everyday space of Paris from static to haptic space. Similar to the ways in which Steven Frear's *Dirty Pretty Things* (2002) and Robert Altman's *Gosford Park* (2001) illustrate how the stable image of the hotel and upper-class home require the invisibility of complex networks of struggle, between immigrants working in the more underground spaces of the hotel and city (*Dirty Pretty Things*), or the visibility of class distinctions through social codes of behavior and dress in the architectural assemblage of the bourgeois home (*Gosford Park*), *Caché* illustrates how the image of a cohesive French culture in Paris, exemplified by the upper-class home in the film, demands the erasure of France's colonialist history. Haneke wants to resist aberrations in time that normalize ideas of a concrete, coherent "colonial time" and instead position one's present understandings of the self as historical conditions of the present. This film thinks accordingly with its understanding "that there is no other crime than time itself" or that representations of "present" time (i.e. colonial time) uniformed by historical and hence political conditions of experience constitute ongoing forms of violence (Deleuze 1989, p. 37).

Navigating the Home Space

Haneke's film debuted in October 2005, roughly one month prior to the riots that erupted in Paris's projects in reaction to massive unemployment amongst many immigrants, and the accidental killing of two teenage immigrant boys by police in Clichy-sous-Bois, and a few months after the implementation of the French law which designated that the "positive role" of French colonial history be implemented into academic curricula, a law led by the then Interior Minister Nicolas Sarkozy (Liauzu 2005). Three months prior to the riots, an article entitled "Suburbs: A Colonial Problem?"[3] (Lancelin & Vigoureux 2005) was issued in a French weekly newspaper, which reported on resistance groups to French colonialism and the disparate economic conditions of many immigrants living in French projects. The article, Robert Aldrich writes:

> reported on the activities of a group who called themselves *les indigènes de la République*, the "Republic's indigenes", mostly descendants of migrants from France's former colonies in North Africa and sub-Saharan Africa. The group ... issued a manifesto demanding redress of their grievances of cultural discrimination, economic exploitation and social disenfranchisement: "The Republic of equality does not exist ... Our parents and grandparents were reduced to slavery ... We, the daughters and sons of colonised peoples and immigrants, are engaged in a struggle against oppression and the discrimination produced by the post-colonial Republic". The inchoately formulated proclamation and provocative initiatives of the organisation attracted little support, even from intellectuals and public figures normally supportive of anti-racist campaigns. (Aldrich 2006, p. 1)

The silence surrounding the resistance to millions of immigrants' current economic and social conditions by intellectuals and politicians in France was made visible in the riots, where nearly 7000 cars were set ablaze in Parisian streets only two weeks after the riots began on 27 October 2005 (see Landler 2005). Commenting in the *New York Times* on the riots, Michel Wieviorka, a French sociologist, points to the symbolic significance of the burning of the cars in Paris's suburban streets. "[W]recking cars", he suggests, "speaks to more than a simple urge to deface property or demand attention. Cars offer — and symbolize — mobility ... something the residents of these projects lack in French society" (Landler 2005).

Significantly, *Caché* turns to the social and political space of the home and street in Paris as central sites of concern in the film, which serve as sites to investigate the economic and social conditions surrounding the immigrant subject and colonialism's past and present in Paris. Haneke brings the viewer through a Paris of enclosed and empty spaces, empty streets, quiet houses and apartment buildings, still images, gated corridors, long, empty hallways and closed doors. The very absence of a hustling Parisian city life, street walkers and cafés in the film functions as a magnifying glass that allows Haneke to bring into focus his central characters and the viewer's own sense of being one amongst the few characters in the film "site-seeing" the enclosed, empty spaces of Paris. Recalling Eisenstein, Haneke only allows the viewer to "see" each character in the film as

---

3. Here I heed Robert Aldrich's English translation of the article's original title, "Banlieues: le mal des colonies?" See Aldrich 2006 for details.

s/he is positioned within an isolated city space (i.e. apartment space, automobile space, window space, street space) or particular social encounter structured by that architectural city space (i.e. Majid's apartment, Anne and Georges's living room), enacting architectural space as that which *constitutes* rather than represents bodies and perception (Eisenstein 1989, p. 113). The film's assemblage of buildings and the spatial arrangement of Paris operate within such an architectural assemblage that thinks by strategically positioning the privacy of the home as an *isolated* space from others and public spaces (faces) of visibility. Isolating the home space allows us to become a *voyageur* to its "hidden" historical presents.

For example, Georges's childhood home, a large estate in a tranquil French country scene, functions as a scene of violence and trauma as an investigation into Majid's departure from the estate as a child unfolds. As noted, Majid is the son of an Algerian family whom Georges's parents planned to adopt following the Algerian War, until he was sent away, a victim of Georges's resentment. Through a series of flashbacks, or possibly nightmares and hallucinations, the scene of Georges's violence toward Majid unfolds outside the home in a small shed facing the estate's aesthetic grandness. Through several reverse-shot sequences, Georges decapitates a farm chicken in the shed, which begins to frolic about frantically. At this point, the camera focuses on Georges and the blood from Majid's positioning in the shed. A reverse shot then centers on the young, terrified Majid who watches Georges with the bloody axe. Then, in another reverse shot, the camera moves back to Georges's gaze as he approaches Majid menacingly with the axe. As Georges raises the axe, the scene cuts, all the while rendering invisible Majid's face. The three shots that dramatize this scene foreground the camera's gaze as a third space or character in the film. This third space of the camera's gaze is that which is able to frame the vision of two figural tropes in this scene, which will reoccur in the next two following scenes — that of the colonizer and the colonized — two figures, that is, which are not essential identities but those constituted by the gaze; in particular, the gaze of the colonizer.

In the following scenes, the home space again reveals the hidden territorializations of violence and turns to colonialism's present histories in Majid's rundown apartment complex. Georges is certain that Majid is the sender of the video-surveillance footage and drawings, and visits Majid's apartment located in the projects. It is clear from his tentative and unsure movements that Georges is not a frequent visitor to the neighboring area. After he enters the apartment, Majid sits at the kitchen table against the wall while Georges stands above him. This appearance of the family table constitutes a moment of referential montage, recalling the scene of one in Georges's upper-bourgeois home. The showing of the two tables effectively juxtaposes the differences between the theatrical display of the Parisian bourgeoisie family and the hidden poverty in France, a legacy of colonialism. "There are always lines in the interior within the apparently safe confines of the house", Beatriz Colomina writes. "Even before we step outside we are engaged in battle. As we all know but rarely publicize, the house is a scene of conflict. The domestic has always been at war" (Colomina

2007, p. 296). As a series of recurrent images of domestic colonial war, Georges's postural stance above Majid at the kitchen table recalls Georges's violent walk toward Majid in the open shed as a child. Again, through several reverse shots, the camera goes back and forth between Georges's and Majid's gaze; each looking back at the other, though Georges is clearly positioned as the dominant figure as in the first scene sequence. Georges's insistence that Majid is the sender of the tapes and drawings, without any evidence or investigatory clues, reaffirms a sort of "haunting" of the dangerous individual in colonialism's persistent imaginaries — willed knowledge of the "other" required in colonialist rhetoric and a national subconscious in order for the processes of colonization to remain unchallenged. "Confronted", Fanon writes, "with a world configured by the colonizer, the colonized subject is always presumed guilty" (Fanon 2004, p. 16). Georges's persistent haunting and belief that Majid is the vengeful stalker, in that Majid is literally "caught" before he is able to defend his "innocence", functions in the film as a rhythmic persistence — a persistence in colonialist thought *à la* Rancière that totalizes difference into a unitary imaginary of the other.

After visiting Majid several times in his apartment, Georges receives a video recording, again from an anonymous sender, this time of a distressed and sullen Majid sitting at his kitchen table. The video recording is footage from Georges's last visit to Majid's apartment as detailed above. It is crucial to note that this video is taken by an unknown other who is standing behind both Georges and Majid against the kitchen wall recording their encounter. Now the gaze of the camera opens up a third space in order to reframe the way in which the first encounter was made visible to the viewer and, undoubtedly, to Georges as he now watches it on his home television screen. Whereas Georges's dominating postural stance above Majid, along with his insistence that he is the vengeful stalker, turns Majid into a spectacle of the other's gaze, the gaze of the camera now turns the encounter into a spectacle and, most importantly, the spectacle of Georges. The camera, as Kaja Silverman might put it, "takes" Georges "from behind" in the domain of the specular, positioning Georges's aversion to an accounting of his wilful gaze of the "other" as a sort of "backstage" violence now center stage (Silverman 1996, p. 65). Georges's insistence that Majid is the vengeful stalker is made the central problematic as now Georges, and the viewer, must determine who is recording the encounter. Is the camera set up by Majid? Is the hidden camera Majid's son? Is it someone else, unknown to both Majid and Georges? The answer to these questions is less important than the disruptions that the questions evoke. The third space of the camera makes Georges and the cinematic spectator think about the ways in which the dominant imaginary of Majid as a threat is necessitated by the mediations of the gaze, which impose an "insistently dyadic logic through which the imaginary articulates the interactions of self and other" (Silverman 1996, p. 65). Several scenes later, Majid asks Georges to visit his apartment. Entering Majid's kitchen, Majid turns to Georges and says, "I wanted you to be present". Majid then slits his own throat. Both these scenes — the spectacle of Georges and Majid's encounter and Majid's death in front of Georges — displace the televisual space of the home and the news media's "war on terror" to another war: a war that has been enacted in the "private" space of the home and a war over public visibility of these hidden violences. The desire to make Majid an object of knowledge, in these terms, is itself an act of violence that extends to the processes by which these persistent visions of the other come to be constituted. As such, the resemblance between the cutting-off of the chicken's head and Majid's suicide functions not necessarily as a representational act of death of the colonized by the colonizer. Rather, the resemblance between the two deaths functions as a time-image where Majid does not simply sacrifice his life because of an impulse produced by the immediate situation, but because of a history of colonialist violence and effacement that has been systematically and structurally imposed upon him since his childhood.

Private and Public Matters

Whether or not Majid is the actual sender of the packages is less important than the ways in which the packages force Georges and the viewer to enter the private space of the home, where the economic and social disparities that have conditioned Majid's present despair are excluded in national narratives on French colonialism. This is particularly the case in present-day Paris where, as noted, the state attempts to position the "positive" aspects of French colonialism and inhibit the politicization of economic and political inequities that condition the present experience of many immigrants.

Hannah Arendt's political topography is instructive in this context. For Arendt, the private realm is historically understood as a place of privacy or as the "hiding place from the common public realm", where private property, for instance, functions as "a privately owned place to hide in" (Arendt 1958, p. 71). Meanwhile, the public realm is defined by a sense of publicity, where "appearance — something that is being seen and heard by others as well as by ourselves — constitutes reality" (p. 50). The public realm is a common world which has its own sense of worldliness: "public" is understood as that which "is common to all of us and *distinguished* from our privately owned place in it", or that which "gathers us together and yet prevents our falling over each other" (p. 52; my emphasis).

As Arendt argues, modernity has witnessed a submersion of the private and public in the sphere of the social, wherein "both the public and private spheres of life are gone, the public because it has become a function of the private and the private because it has become the only common concern left" (p. 69). This submersion of the public and private realms in the social depoliticizes man's relationship to the other in the public realm. She writes:

> To live an entirely private life means above all to be deprived of things essential to a truly human life: to be deprived of the reality that comes from being seen and heard from others, to be deprived of an "objective" relationship with them that comes from being related to and separated from them through the intermediary of a common world of things, to be deprived of the possibility of achieving something more permanent than life itself. *The privation of privacy lies in the*

absence of others; as far as they are concerned, private man does not appear, and therefore it is as though he does not exist. Whatever he does remains without significance and consequence to others, and what matters to him is without interest to other people. (Arendt 1958, p. 58)

This is why it is so important for Arendt, as she puts it in *The Human Condition*, that political action take place in the public realm, where it will retain its visibility and not be exiled to the dark shadows of the private (non-privative private). What is interesting, then, in *Caché* is the way in which the anonymous tapes sent to Georges bring Georges into the privacy of Majid's home, wherein the "privation of privacy" — that which "lies in the absence of others" — is disrupted by the intervention of Majid into Georges's social space and the entrance of Georges into Majid's lifeworld through the route of the *private* social space of the home. The entrance of Georges into Majid's lifeworld and of Majid into Georges's via the private home space is brilliantly illuminated in the key scene described earlier when Georges first visits Majid at his apartment. While Georges presses Majid to confess as to why he is presumably stalking his family, Majid replies, "Why do you talk like we're strangers? You wouldn't have recognized me, huh? Outside, you'd have walked right past me." Majid then emphasizes Georges's public visibility as a popular talk-show host and national media figure, and Georges's connection to the public via the televisual space of the home: "When I tuned into your show by chance, a few years ago," Majid says to Georges, "You sat up close to your guests, face to face ... I felt nauseous and I didn't know why. When your name came up, I began to understand." Majid's emphasis on his invisibility to Georges on the streets of Paris, as a "private man" living in the *banlieues*, is important. Majid's statement on his social invisibility (to Georges and the viewer) reflects Arendt's emphasis that Majid "does not exist" in the submersion of the private and the public in the social. Yet, at the same time, this scene reframes the notion of private space as a space that "lies in the absence of others", in Arendtian terms, to a private/public, inside/outside space where face-to-face conversations with the nation, through Georges's television talk show, are imagined and realized. As a significant rearticulation of Arendt's emphasis on the public realm as the only space where politics might be realized (through the visibility of political action), this scene positions the dark shadows of the private home space (and not the open streets of Paris) as the site where Majid is finally able to respond to Georges's public media gaze and, literally, be "seen" by Georges. More significantly, in this scene it is in the private space of the home that the "public" viewing audience is able to "see" Majid, where the notion of "being seen" and constituting Majid as an object of knowledge is later interrupted by the fact that this encounter is being taped by an anonymous viewer, further disrupting the notion of the private sphere as a neutrally-charged site of social control.

Arendt's understandings of the public and private realms thus help us approach the significance of the ways in which the "public" media functions in relationship to the "privacy" of the home. The lack of distinction between the spectator and spectacle in *Caché* is illuminated, for example, by the juxtaposition of both the family home and media space as places of national performativity and systems of control. While the home is typically narrated as a familial (feminine) space of privacy, and the media as a mass form of (masculine) publicity, Haneke attempts to dismantle these two distinctions into their more nuanced contemporary facets. He illuminates the ways in which national ideas of the family proper, a concept inherent to French colonial policies, are imagined not only in the public media realm, but also in the private spaces of the home.[4] By illustrating the ways in which national ideas of the French family are deployed in both public and private spaces, Haneke challenges Arendt's political topography that ultimately demands a clear demarcation between the public and private spheres. This subtle move is made evident in the film by the recurrence of objects from Georges and Anne's family table in Georges's talk-show set. A bookshelf, for example, stands as a set-like wall in both Anne and Georges's dining room and on Georges's talk-show set.

While the dining room in the home (see Figure 1) is cast as a theatrical set to forge intimate connections with friends and family, the family-like living room of the talk-show set also functions as a theatrical stage to forge intimate connections with the friends and family of the nation (see Figure 2). Both theatrical scenes thus position the "public" as well as the "private" as spectacles of theatricality — mediated by the necessity of an anonymous "public" spectator (for example, even the "you" and the "I" as we watch the film). Theatricality, in these terms, functions less as an anomaly between the public and private, but rather as an affirmation of their *interdependence* and mutually co-extensive forms of mediating an abstract sense of national familial intimacy.

---

4. We can better understand how French colonial policies are largely informed by national republican ideas of the 'proper' family if we pay attention to Mustafa Dikeç's emphasis on the increased role of the 'republican penal state' in recent French urban policy developments. In his article 'Two Decades of French Urban Policy: From Social Development of Neighbourhoods to the Republican Penal State', Dikeç traces the ways in which neo-liberal urban policy initiatives have played a contradictory role in urban policy development from the 1980s and 1990s. As Dikeç makes clear, urban policies in the 1980s were characterized by a quasi-neo-liberal reform agenda and a general discourse of republican nationalism. However, in the 1990s the state began to play a larger role in urban policy strategies at the same time that discourses surrounding 'ideals of the Republic' and republican nationalisms heightened. The increased role of the state in urban policy strategies, Dikeç stresses, is legitimized by the state's insistence that it must manage (i.e. through surveillance apparatuses) the 'dangerous' peripheral areas of the cities (i.e. the ghettoes). 'While there have been attempts to re-orient urban policy', Dikeç writes, 'towards the extension of the market relations, the main determinant factor ... has remained that of the republican tradition with its emphasis on the responsibility of the state to maintain "social cohesion" with increasingly authoritarian measures' (Dikeç 2006, p. 69). Thus, while republican ideals informing French urban policy affirm a national, cohesive republic (i.e. national family) in opposition to a cohesive, dangerous 'otherness' of the *banlieues*, Haneke emphasizes, as I will illustrate, the ways in which these national ideas of the republic that inform colonial urban policies are performative, contestable and highly mediated operations of social control, enacted in the public and private spheres. By rendering the 'public' media and the 'private' space of the home as mutually defining apparatuses of meaning making — as a site where *a nation of abstract others* is materialized — Haneke directly challenges French (colonial) urban policy discourses that necessitate the very notion of an abstract 'otherness' (i.e. the otherness of the ghettos) in their discursive formations.

Figure 1 Familial space in the Laurent dining room and bookshelf.

Juxtaposing the talk show and home space, then, and their similar spaces of appearance in the realm of the social, collapses the sharp distinction between the public space of the media and the private realm of the home. At the same time, this juxtaposition of public and private media spaces, such as the talk-show set and the home's televisual screen, illuminates the ways in which media technologies operate in the public and private realm to create a national familial intimacy of disconnected, abstract others. Perhaps Arendt might then argue that what counts as "relevant" politics is not the everyday complexities of individual lives, such as Majid's, but the constant array of media images transmitted into the privacy of one's home. As mentioned earlier, according to Arendt's understanding, the private realm, as "the only common concern left" now with the submersion of the private and public spheres in the social, retains a visibility in the public realm, which is the only thing that matters: in this case, an abstract sense of familial intimacy disconnected from the real, concrete experience of everyday life. This selective visibility of people's everyday life in the public realm also suggests that we should remain cautious of the ways in which the "spectacle" is presented as a moment of rupture in the "public" realm, such as the outbreak of violence in Paris in November 2005, and the ways in which these spectacles are consumed by the social, as distinct from the more "hidden" complexities that are relegated as private matters.

Figure 2 Familial space and bookshelf on George's talk-show set.

Inside and Outside Space

The juxtaposition of the home space with the media space is also illuminated in the film through the architectural construction of Georges and Anne's house itself. This juxtaposing effect of private and public spaces through the architectural assemblage of the home space in the film becomes evident if we heed Beatriz Colomina's thesis that modern architecture *is* media space.[5] Colomina sketches the architectural politics of two prominent twentieth-century architects, Loos and Le Corbusier, to unearth the ways in which architectural media functions. The assemblages of Loos' home space, she illustrates, were created as stages or as "theater boxes" where the furniture, objects, windows and walls were constructed to create a space of both "intimacy and control" (Colomina 1992, p. 76). It is in this sense that "architecture", she writes, "is not simply a

---

5. For a more detailed discussion on modern architecture as media, see Colomina (1994). Here, Colomina turns to the ways in which modern architecture functions as a system of representation within modern forms of mass culture. Approaching architecture, she writes, as a 'high artistic practice established in position to mass culture and to everyday life' grossly overlooks the ways in which modern architecture and the mass media mutually define each other. Modern architecture is therefore *not* similar to the media or vice versa. Instead, she argues, 'modern architecture only becomes modern with its engagement with the media' (Colomina 1994, p. 14).

platform that accommodates the viewing subject. It is a viewing mechanism that produces the subject. It precedes and frames its occupant" (p. 83). For example, in Loos' Moller House, the window functions not as a frame to capture the outside world but only as a source of light. In order to have a view of the exterior from inside the house, one's eye must first travel the interior living spaces of the home that open onto the back garden: "The exterior view depends upon a view of the interior" (p. 78). In the Steiner House, moreover, the mirrors (placed at eye level) function as windows that return the gaze back to the interior of the dining-room space. It is in this sense that the arrangement of the house functions as an architectural device of capture. On this domestic stage, the stage actor's gaze is thrown back onto the self and interior space depending on one's positioning in the house. Loosian architecture thus disrupts dominant understandings of the home as an object and constructs the home instead as a viewing space, where binary distinctions between the inside and outside space of the home are dislodged by "radically convoluting the relation between inside and outside" (Colomina 1992, p. 85).

On the other hand, Le Corbusier's houses enact a reverse of the Loosian interior gaze. In these homes, the gaze is directed not toward the interior of the home but toward the exterior and outside space of the house. In the Le Corbusierian house, the horizontal window (rather than Loos' vertical windows) functions, for example, as a contested frame that is positioned in order to capture a fracture of the landscape view. It is in this sense that the Le Corbusierian subject who enters the home no longer "looks" out at the outside landscape but rather "sees" a defined exterior that has been noticeably constructed to give a glimpse of a particular view. As Colomina puts it, Le Corbusier's houses — "where the outside is always the inside" — suggest that "to inhabit" the domestic space of the home "means to see", disrupting the distinctions between looking and seeing, landscape and site, inside and outside (Colomina 1992, p. 125). These disruptions are similar to the ambiguities of looking and seeing in cinematic montage as well, constituting the Le Corbusierian subject more as a movie actor or "moving visitor" than the stage actor of Loos' subject (p. 114).

Significantly, in *Caché*, Haneke incorporates both a Loosian and Le Corbusierian understanding of the outside/inside of the gaze. The mirror in Georges and Anne's living room, for example, functions as a Loosian window that constantly returns the gaze to the interior domestic space of the home. Furthermore, the windows that we are allowed to see in the house fail to capture the exterior view of the home. Rather, the home and familial space are hidden from the seemingly threatening world outside, including the sender of the surveillance footage. The window in Georges's bedroom, moreover, functions as a reflection image of his past, reflecting the image of him as a young boy. The bedroom window in this sense functions more as a media space — as well as a temporal frame that oscillates between the past and present — than as a functional frame to capture an exterior view from the home. At the same time, Haneke incorporates a Le Corbusierian view of the home by incorporating the media space of Georges's talk show into the interior of the home: "the outside is always the inside". This effect is also enacted by the long horizontal window that is placed at the top of the house, allowing a submarine-like view of the outside landscape, capturing a brief view of the city street.

As illustrated earlier, collapsing the distinctions between private and public space, and inside and outside space is important, because it is the very interdependence of these supposedly separate spheres/spaces that mediates national ideas of the French family proper inherent to colonial policies (i.e. urban colonial policies). Recalling Arendt's treatment of the relationship between the public and private realms, the architectural assemblage of the home in the film, narrated in both Loosian and Le Corbusierian understandings of the interior/exterior, inside/outside construction of space, disrupts the ultimate distinction that Arendt makes between the public and private sphere. To elaborate on Bruno's approach to the distinctions between the cinematic viewer as a voyeur and as a voyager as, at best, conflicting demarcations, the construction of Anne and Georges's home situates the viewer as both a voyeur in the (Loosian) stage theater and as a voyager or "moving visitor" in the (Le Corbusierian) cinematic space of movement. By politicizing more dominant political boundaries/borders between public and private space in the home itself, Haneke's film offers a radical critique on the privation of privacy and modern architecture as media.

Conclusion

Whereas in *La Haine* each character is confronted daily with police brutality and surveillance, in *Caché* the viewer is solicited to think about the ways in which national ideas of the French "family", "security" and immigrant "other" are highly policed categories of knowledge enacted, in part, through the individual. Haneke demands that the viewer critically question the historical conditions as to why Georges insists that he has "caught" Majid as the culprit and as an object of knowledge. Writing on the moral twist in Dickens's novel *Oliver Twist*, D. A. Miller provides observations that are instructive here. He highlights the ways in which the policing of delinquency represented in *Oliver Twist* is structured to emphasize the violence of making Oliver an object of knowledge. "To constitute Oliver", he writes, "as an object of knowledge is thus to assume power over him as well" (Miller 1989, p. 133). Perhaps this is why Haneke refuses to leave the viewer with knowledge of who the real "culprit" is, of who is actually sending the surveillance footage. Rather, Haneke chooses to leave the viewer with the gaze of the camera that zooms in on the scene of Majid's and Georges's sons after school. Unlike the detective or police novel, the "culprit" in the film is rather the particular, more "hidden" ways in which vision and perception of the self and other in colonial imaginaries are structured in the historical present of Paris.

The "hidden" absence of police in Haneke's Paris, as compared to *La Haine*, foregrounds the role of the media and architecture (or architecture as media) as policing apparatuses operating in societies of control. The continuous gaze *as* culprit throughout the film reinforces the often invisible mechanics of disciplinary power — such as the gaze or distinction between the private and public — as that which "constitutively mobilizes a tactic of tact: it is the power that never passes as such, either invisible or visible only under cover of other intentionalities" (Miller 1989, p. 138). By foregrounding the ways in which colonial violences are enacted through these more subtle policing apparatuses in societies of control — such as the distinction between the self and other in colonial imaginaries, enacted, in part, through the individual — the film offers an important counter-narrative of the state's desire to depoliticize the continuation of colonial practices in the present. It provides an important example of the multiple ways in which the city space of Paris might be articulated within a political sensibility sensitive to the more "hidden", subtle practices of colonialism's ongoing violences.

Acknowledgement

I would like to extend my thanks to Michael J. Shapiro for his extremely helpful suggestions and encouraging comments on earlier versions of this article.

References

Aldrich, R. (2006) 'Colonial Past, Post-colonial Present: History Wars French Style', *History Australia*, vol. 3, no. 1, pp. 1-10, http://publications/epress/monash.edu/doi/10.2104/ha060014.

Arendt, H. (1958) *The Human Condition*, University of Chicago Press, Chicago, IL.

BBC News (2002) 'Profile: Jean-Marie Le Pen', 23 April, http://news.bbc.co.uk/2/low/europe/1943193.stm.

BBC News (2006) 'Chirac Warns of "African Flood"', 14 July, http://news.bbc.co.uk/2/hi/europe/5181080.stm.

Benjamin, W. (2002) *The Arcades Project*, ed. Tiedemann, R., trans. Eiland, H. and McLaughlin, K., Belknap Press, Cambridge, MA.

Benjamin, W. (2006) *The Writer of Modern Life: Essays on Charles Baudelaire*, The Belknap Press of Harvard University Press, Cambridge, MA.

Bois, Y.-A. (1989) 'Presentation of the text by S. M. E. Eisenstein, "Montage and architecture"', *Assemblage*, vol. 10, pp. 111-115.

Bruno, G. (1997) 'Site-seeing: Architecture and the Moving Image', *Wide Angle*, vol. 19, no. 4, pp. 8-24.

Chirac, J. (2005) 'Speech by Jacques Chirac, President of the French Republic, on the occasion of the symposium for a Europe of Culture', *Archives of Jacques Chirac's Presidency 1995—2007*, 2 May, http://www.elysee.fr/elysee/elysee.fr/anglais_archives/speeches_and_documents/2005/2005_speeches_and_documents.27733.html.

Colomina, B. (1992) 'The Split Wall: Domestic Voyeurism', in Colomina, B. (ed.) *Sexuality and Space*, Princeton Architectural Press, Princeton, NJ.

Colomina, B. (1994) *Privacy and Publicity: Modern Architecture as Mass Media*, The MIT Press, Cambridge, MA.

Colomina, B. (2007) *Domesticity at War*, The MIT Press, Cambridge, MA.

Deleuze, G. (1989) *Cinema 2: The Time-Image*, University of Minnesota Press, Minneapolis, MN.

Deleuze, G. (1992) 'Postscript on the Societies of Control', *October*, no. 59, Winter, pp. 3-7.
Dikeç, M. (2006) 'Two Decades of French Urban Policy: From Social Development of Neighbourhoods to the Republican Penal State', *Antipode*, vol. 38, no. 1, pp. 59-81.
Eisenstein, S. M. (1989) 'Montage and Architecture', with an introduction by Y.-A. Bois, *Assemblage*, no. 10, pp. 110-131.
Fanon, F. (2004) *The Wretched of the Earth*, Grove Press, New York.
Foucault, M. (2003) *'Society Must Be Defended': Lectures at the Collège de France, 1975-1976*, trans. Macey, D., Picador, New York.
Kimmelman, M. (2007) 'Ready or Not, France Opens Museum on Immigration', *The New York Times*, 17 October, http://www.nytimes.com/2007/10/17/arts/design/17abroad.html.
Lancelin, A. & Vigoureux, E. (2005) 'Banlieues: les mal des colonies?' *Le Nouvel Observateur*, 23 June, http://hebdo.nouvelobs.com/hebdo/parution/p2120/articles/a271922-.html.
Landler, M. (2005) 'A Very French Message from the Disaffected', *The New York Times*, 13 November, http://www.nytimes.com/2005/11/13/international/europe/13cars.html.
Liauzu, C. (2005) 'At War with France's Past', *Le Monde diplomatique*, June, http://mondediplo.com/2005/06/19colonisation.
Miller, D. A. (1989) *The Novel and the Police*, University of California Press, Berkeley, CA.
Payeur, P. & Elhadad, L. (2007) 'Landmarks — A Permanent Exhibition: 200 Years of Immigration', *Museum International*, vol. 59, no. 1-2, pp. 73-79.
Rancière, J. (1995) *On the Shores of Politics*, trans. Heron, L., Verso, London.
Rancière, J. (2004) *The Politics of Aesthetics: The Distribution of the Sensible*, trans. & introd. Rockhill, G., Continuum, London.
Silverman, K. (1996) *The Threshold of the Visible*, Routledge, New York.
Vidler, A. (2002) 'Metropolitan Montage: The City as Film in Kracauer, Benjamin, and Eisenstein', in *Warped Space: Art, Architecture, and Anxiety in Modern Culture*, The MIT Press, Cambridge, MA.

Crossing the Border: Art and Change in East Harlem

Allison Pan

Too easily subsumed by its greater neighbor Harlem and dwarfed by larger minority populations in the other boroughs including the Bronx, East Harlem has all but disappeared from the collective memory. This paper tries to recover East Harlem, also known as Spanish Harlem or El Barrio, from its public obscurity and reclaim its importance as a vital urban center in the fabric of Manhattan life. East Harlem is comprised of a rich collection of people from multiple ethnic, economic, and social backgrounds and it is they who provide the backdrop for my analysis of the political life of the neighborhood. The nature of political life in East Harlem is to be found not in the traditional sphere of the political — the acquisition and distribution of power — but in the intersections of the lives of its diverse inhabitants and the articulation of individual and collective assertiveness. I hope to understand and elucidate the composite narratives of urban life in East Harlem through a reading of urban art: architecture, street art, private home design, and photographic documentation of the neighborhood. The aesthetic representations of East Harlem can provide the same insight into the narratives of the neighborhood's life worlds and life stories as biographical profiles of the inhabitants.

I have always found Jennifer Lopez's album *On the 6* more than a little disingenuous. Touting her album as a tribute to her upbringing in the Bronx, which is connected to Manhattan by the number 6 train of New York's subway system, Lopez hoped the album, through its title, would artistically reconnect her to her roots. When I first learned of Lopez's album title, in 1999, I was intrigued. For me, and other veteran 6 train riders, the 6 was the only subway line dedicated to the service of East Harlem. Harlem, with its access to express stops and thus the 4, 5, and the West Side lines 1, 2, 3, and 9, not to mention a Metro North station, has many other subway options. The Bronx also has a variety of subway options, many shared with Harlem by virtue of its geographic proximity to the Bronx. East Harlem, however, has only the 6 train, stopping at 96th, 103rd, 110th, 116th, and 125th Streets, the first and last of those being the southern and northern boundaries of East Harlem, respectively. The 6 belongs to the Bronx no more than bodegas belong to the Upper East Side, home to two of America's richest zip codes, 10028 and 10128 (Clemence 2005).

The appropriation of East Harlem's own subway line by the already more politically vocal and dominant Bronx is an affront to East Harlemites; Lopez's claim, and the silent approval of the New York community, is tantamount not just to geospatial imperialism but, to a large degree, is representative of the daily omission of the unique character of East Harlem from the public conscience. Too easily subsumed by its greater neighbor Harlem and dwarfed by larger minority populations in the other boroughs including the Bronx, East Harlem, my childhood home, has all but disappeared from the collective memory. This article will seek to recover East Harlem, also known as Spanish Harlem or El Barrio, from its public obscurity and reclaim its importance as a vital urban center in the fabric of Manhattan life.

East Harlem is one of the smaller neighborhoods in Manhattan but because of its nominal and geographical proximity to the more famous, and politically influential, Harlem, is regularly ignored as its own separate neighborhood, with a pace and vitality unique to life within its boundaries. Topographically, those boundaries have remained much the same for nearly a century; East Harlem's northern boundary is East 125th Street, its southern limit is East 96th Street, and Central Park/5th Avenue and the East River are its western and eastern limits, respectively (Sharman 2006, p. xi). Though the neighborhood is commonly known as Spanish Harlem, that designation is only about 50 years old and coincides with the mass migration of Puerto Ricans to New York following World War II. Urban centers drew most of the Puerto Rican immigrants in the late 1940s through the 1960s, with New York's then Little Italy drawing the greatest share of the numbers (Sharman 2006, p. 5). That East Harlem was once New York's Little Italy or Italian Harlem, and prior to that host to communities of German, Irish, and Jewish immigrants, should not be a particular surprise to anyone familiar with the diversity of the city (Sharman 2006, p. xi). Neither should the fact that Chinese, Africans, Caribbeans, Europeans, and upwardly mobile professionals (mostly white) are increasingly common faces seen on the streets of the neighborhood. But it is. Largely because of the popularization of "El Barrio" and the more popular reference to the neighborhood as "Spanish Harlem", the neighborhood is still routinely associated with only Puerto Ricans and their Hispanic culture.

This association of contemporary twenty-first-century East Harlem with only Puerto Rican life stands in stark opposition to the realities of the area today. The Hispanic population in the neighborhood is no longer singularly Puerto Rican — Mexicans are not only the second largest group of Hispanics in the area, but they will very likely outnumber Puerto Ricans soon. Other Latino groups are also visible in the area: Dominicans, Ecuadorians, and Cubans fly their flags from their windows and cars as proudly as the Puerto Ricans. Hispanics are not even the largest minority group in the area; non-Hispanic black Americans now comprise a majority of the population in Spanish Harlem (Sharman 2006, p. 15). West Africans and immigrants from the Caribbean are also increasingly visible. Chinese American families began settling in the area in the late 1950s and are still trickling in today. And finally, the young professionals, the latest group to begin their movement into East Harlem, are slowly moving into East Harlem because they are being pushed out of better neighborhoods downtown by soaring real estate prices. French patisseries and bistros, expensive steakhouses, and luxury condos, in addition to the more obvious telltale signs, such as Caucasians who look like they might not actually be lost, are only some of the indicators of this new group beginning to call East Harlem home. This rich collection of people from multiple ethnic, economic, and social backgrounds provides the backdrop for my analysis of the political life of East Harlem.

To think of East Harlem as a home to such a population requires, first of all, a clarified understanding of that elusive term "home". Jamaica Kincaid (1999, p. 30) writes that "a house has a physical definition; a home has a spiritual one". But why is this so? Witold Rybczynski's treatise on the historical development of the notion of "the home" informs us that while physical dwellings have sheltered human beings since time immemorial, the transformation of a physical place into that spiritual idea of a home, particularly the family home, begins only with the emergence of the "private home and family life" (1986, p. 59). Thus, the idea of a house belonging to a specific family requires that the family understand itself as a separate unit from the public domain. Such an idea — that of a private sphere separate from the public — required, according to Rybczynski, a critical mass of bourgeois families, particularly within the large urban centers of medieval Europe (p. 25). As more and more families adopted this sense of private space, their homes acquired an "atmosphere of domesticity that is the result of human activity", so that each home reflected the family within (Rybczynski 1986, p. 43). Eventually, the idea of the home evolved to the point where Kincaid can claim, confidently, that her family is settled, "for that sort of settling down is an external metaphor for something that should be done inside, a restfulness, so that you can concentrate on this other business, living, bringing up a child" (1999, p. 30). The family belongs to the home in spirit just as the house belongs to the family in legality. How fitting, then, for our discussion of a neighborhood in one of the largest urban centers of the world, that the notion of a home historically began not in an idyllic pastoral setting but rather within the specific context of urban politics.

The very diversity of East Harlem makes it an example of "the global city" simply because it is a "new frontier zone where an enormous mix of people converge" (Sassen 2003, p. 25). The diverse community of East Harlem shares a common space but each group has very different experiences within that shared existence. In her treatment of the political economy of global cities, Saskia Sassen notes that these locations are traditionally areas that house "those who lack power — those who are disadvantaged, who are outsiders", but once established in the global city, they "gain presence vis-à-vis power and presence vis-à-vis each other". She reads the transformation of the disenfranchised into the enfranchised as a signal of "the possibility of a new type of politics centered in new types of political actors". She explains that "[i]t is not simply a matter of having or not having power. There are new hybrid bases from which to act" (p. 25).

To accommodate Sassen's call for the recognition of new political actors and movements, we must seek out new methods for reading the city. Indeed, the story of poor, disadvantaged immigrant communities moving into East Harlem, only to slowly move out as they accumulate both wealth and social status while being replaced by a new group of the disadvantaged, is repeated from the original exodus of the German and Jewish New Yorkers to make way for the Italians, to the Puerto Rican displacement of the Italians, the gradual migration of Puerto Ricans away from East Harlem, and the influx of the new faces that define the neighborhood's diversity today (Sharman 2006, p. 77). Recalling Jacques Rancière's (2006) claim that "politics is first of all ... the framing of a specific sphere of experience, the setting of objects posed as 'common' and ... the conflict about the very existence of that sphere of existence, the reality of those common objects and the capacity of these objects", the nature of political life in East Harlem, then, is to be found not in the traditional sphere of the political — the acquisition and distribution of power — but in the intersections of the "life stories" of its diverse inhabitants and the articulation of individual and collective assertiveness (Sharman 2006, p. 12). Since "much of urban politics is concrete, enacted by people rather than depending on massive media technologies", we must analyze the politics of East Harlem through "street-level politics" that makes possible the "formation of new types of political subjects that do not have to go through the formal political system" (Sharman 2006, p. 25).

Russell Sharman, a cultural anthropologist and self-proclaimed member of the newest of East Harlem's collection of racial backgrounds, the whites, offers one answer on how to read the new politics of the neighborhood. His recently published book *The Tenants of East Harlem* (2006) explores the political life of East Harlem through an anthropological survey of the neighborhood. It also inspired my use of ethnic intersections as the source of understanding political life in East Harlem. The book, through a collection of profiles of a representative sample of the neighborhood's diversity and a monumental documentation of the neighborhood's history starting with the late 1800s, traces East Harlem's "competing narratives of urbanism: one inscribed in concrete and the other in flesh" (Sharman 2006, p. 1). He writes:

> People conform to the built environment just as the built environment conforms to people over the course of generations and centuries. The story of East Harlem is written in the sidewalks and storefronts, the abandoned buildings and corner bodegas, the public school yards and project courtyards as much as it is written in the lives of Puerto Ricans and African Americans, Italians and Mexicans, new immigrants and old. To understand East Harlem, one must understand how these two narratives fit together, how people transform the streets and how the streets transform the people. (Sharman 2006, p. 1)

Like Sharman, I hope to understand and elucidate the composite narratives of urban life in East Harlem. However, unlike him, I hope to accomplish that task through a reading of urban art: architecture, street art, private home design, and photographic documentation of the neighborhood. If, as Rancière (2006) claims, "art empowers a collective life to the extent that it creates a remote and empty space dedicated to individual meditation", then aesthetic representations of

East Harlem can provide the same insight into the narratives of the neighborhood's lifeworlds and life stories as biographical profiles of the inhabitants. As non-traditional artistic representations of life in the city, the genres I have chosen are all demonstrative of art in the everyday. After all, as Dolores Hayden (1995, p. 9) writes, "urban landscapes are storehouses for those social memories, because natural features such as hills or harbors, as well as streets, buildings, and patterns of settlement, frame the lives of many people and often outlast many lifetimes".

Furthermore, such elements offer unique perspectives on the politics of an urban landscape not "owing to the messages and feelings that [they] convey on the state of social and political issues" or by "the way it represents social structures, conflicts, or identities" but "by virtue of the very distance that it takes with respect to those functions" (Rancière 2006). Understanding that the city is uniquely equipped to transmit "a complex culture from generation to generation, for it marshal[s] together not only the physical means but the human agents needed to pass on and enlarge this heritage" (Kittler 2006), the genres I have chosen represent the "invisible passages", "networks", and "open spaces" (ibid.) of the urban landscape that offer critical insights into the "common sensorium" (Rancière 2006) of life in East Harlem, as shared by its "tenants" (Sharman 2006, p. 1).

My readings of the aforementioned genres will be guided by theoretical texts on the city, Sharman's anthropological survey, and by my own experiences of a childhood spent happily in East Harlem. To that end, what might appear to be a very anecdotal approach to documentation is, in fact, a reflection of my aim to inform my readings with personal narratives. The conditions of possibility for my own life are intricately tied to the connections and intersections of lifeworlds within East Harlem: I was born in Shanghai and I moved to East Harlem with my parents at the age of five. I saw the results of converting rent-stabilized public housing into co-op apartments when our building, one of the newer and more "luxury" public housing developments, commonly known as "projects", slowly became privatized. And finally, as a sophomore in high school, I helped my father close a deal on newly-built housing in East Harlem designed to draw middle-income families by offering subsidized ownership of town homes. I also helped draft the first lease agreements that made Russell Sharman and his lovely wife, Cheryl, tenants.

The details of my life, and that of my family, are so intricately interwoven with the "revival" of East Harlem which began in the 1990s that, at times, I catch myself speaking of my life as the life of East Harlem — which could be true to an extent. My story parallels the economic growth occurring in the neighborhood, but the common sensorium that I and many others of my generation share also faces fierce competition from a different set of collective memories — ones that remember a time when Chinese families like mine were not permanent fixtures of the neighborhood and ones that disagree vehemently with our appreciation for the gentrification of the neighborhood. One illustration of where collective memories simultaneously converge and diverge is the Aguilar Branch Public

Library, on East 106th Street between Third and Lexington Avenues. The library was established in 1899 and

> despite its misleading name, is not connected to Puerto Rican settlement. It was named for Grace Aguilar, a poet, theologian, and Sephardic Jew. Jewish organizations from New York's Lower East Side founded the library in East Harlem to serve the growing community of Russian Jews moving north out of their own immigrant ghetto. (Sharman 2006, p. 33)

In the 1930s, the library played protective castle to one of Sharman's profiles, Pete, who remembers running to the library as a 10-year-old when chased by a gang of black youths threatening to steal his skates (Sharman 2006, p. 33). Another East Harlem resident, José, recalls a childhood spent at the Aguilar Library to avoid being left back in school (Sharman 2006, p. 60). Sixty years later, that same library would also play the benevolent host to a young Chinese American girl determined to finish entire sections of the library every summer. She succeeded — finishing the entire children's section when she, like Pete, was 10. That little girl was me. Though Sharman, in his interviews with Pete, the "old guard" and one of the few remaining Italian tenants of East Harlem, does not ask Pete what he thinks of that young girl, and children like her of every ethnic background, who find in the Aguilar Library a refuge from the turmoil of daily urban life, Pete does volunteer his insights about the growing Asian, predominantly Chinese, community "finding" their way to East Harlem. Pete warns rather cryptically against the Chinese entry into East Harlem:

> They'll run you out, like they done on Grand Street. They've been doing it down on Mott Street, too. You're not familiar with Grand Street, what it was like. They took over everything. The same thing would be here. You already got some of them who have been going into Franklin Plaza. They're in there.[1] It's on Second Avenue, it's not a city thing, it's kind of a complex. (Sharman 2006, p. 46)

Despite our shared experiences in the beloved neighborhood public library, Pete clearly does not welcome the presence of Chinese Americans in the community. The library is both a shared memory and a point of departure for consensus, just like East Harlem. We all live in the same area, attend the same schools, ride the same trains. But we have very different visions of what East Harlem is or should be.

Distinct against the "monoliths of public housing"[2], the Aguilar Library building is a stately example of turn-of-the-century American architecture. Its grand,

---

1. Pete is absolutely correct in one respect — about one-third of all families in Franklin Plaza are Chinese. Chinese families living outside Franklin Plaza in the neighborhood, like my parents and I, are still rare. On the other hand, the first Chinese residents of Franklin Plaza, including my great-grandfather who was sponsored by R. J. Reynolds after he worked for and befriended an executive of the company during World War II, have been in the complex since the mid 1950s. My great-grandfather and his family moved there in the 1960s. In other words, the Chinese have been in East Harlem, technically, for almost as long as the Puerto Ricans.
2. This phrase is used by Sharman (2006, p. 51), although it is also frequently encountered elsewhere.

neoclassical style stands in stark contrast to the dejected and forlorn buildings that house the children who visit the library. The library commands attention from pedestrians as they shuffle on their way to the 110th Street subway station at the end of the street. Unlike the ever-changing community that revolves around the library, the building is a testament to ideals that remain strong; ideals that once drew, and still today draw, new residents to the neighborhood. The promise of a safe haven, a public and adequate education as a preliminary step to a better future, and the unflinching calm and stability in a city marked by its dynamism are what one might interpret from its austere, orderly Greco-Roman columns and relief details. The framing of all the windows by the two massive columns suggests that the entire library is a gateway to some unknown, but hopefully better, future. Or, perhaps, as the neighborhood continues to evolve and the landscape of East Harlem keeps changing, from grand brownstones to tenements to high-rise projects to now privately developed and owned town homes, the library is the gateway towards an unchanging past and shared experience. As if architecturally reflecting the generations of children of every background who have patronized the library, the Aguilar Library reminds us that some things never change. Much as Sharman's title suggests, the most obvious of our shared experiences in East Harlem is our temporariness — the residents are just tenants, temporarily passing on their way to the rest of their lives. The faces of the tenants and library-goers change, but East Harlem as a dynamic community does not. And with every new child who visits that grand institution, the library reminds us that "agents are not merely located at a simple point in a grid, but occupy and define the world through the unfolding of practice" (Jordan 2003, p. 31).

While the Aguilar Library has remained an unchanged institution in the community over the last century, the architectural changes to East Harlem's housing landscape tell of another weave in the area's fabric of urban life. Three major types of residential housing dominate the neighborhood: the old tenement buildings of Italian Harlem, the enormous housing projects built in the 1960s and 1970s, and the recent crop of housing developments built and sold by private developers. The grand town houses of Italian Harlem also still stand today but they are mostly dilapidated, vacant, and solemnly awaiting the wrecking ball. The housing projects that began to appear in the 1960s were largely the product of the city's grand vision to produce huge quantities of affordable housing, encased in symmetrical, modern skyscrapers and grouped around idyllic patches of green. Similar projects have sprung up in urban centers around the country; Jennifer Jordan (2003, p. 36) writes that "affordable" housing in San Diego's Barrio Logan was a positive indication of the power of a "shared narrative about the past, present, and future of the neighborhood".

Jordan's is an overly positive reflection on the appearance of urban housing projects, and reflective of what they were *supposed* to be. Perhaps in San Diego they were like this, though her optimistic stance so eerily echoes the same words of buoyant hope when the New York housing projects were first built that one wonders if she too might not recant her words in another 30 or 40 years. Joseph

Rodriguez, born in the 1950s and a long-time resident, author, and photographer of East Harlem, calls the development of low-income housing the "economic death-knell" of East Harlem (Rodriguez 1994, p. 13). His photographs, *Abandoned Building, 1987* and *The Business, 1987*, reflect his sentiments. While the photograph Sharman includes in his book offers a sterile, well-composed, side-by-side comparison of different types of housing — which he aptly captions "Housing, old and new"—, Rodriguez's photographs are harsh and dark, and clearly mourn the disappearance of the East Harlem he was born into but that was consumed by urban planners who themselves had no understanding of the richness and dynamism of the neighborhood. Though the massive housing projects are not the focal point of Rodriguez's compositions, they are the backdrop just as they are in real life; ever present and looming in the background of East Harlem life.

As the daily lives of El Barrio inhabitants unfold on the street, the housing projects are always there, even if not directly in the forefront, as architectural reminders of the neighborhood's collapse since their creation. The orderly appearance of red-brick, small, evenly-spaced windows and a geometry that suggests an eternal reach towards the sky dominate the East Harlem landscape today. These monoliths are usually hideous in their scale — the sad results of executing a plan that incorporates Euclidean geometry at its most sterile and austere. There is not a decorative element to speak of, although perhaps the designers meant the absolute absence of architectural decoration to be a reversal of the traditional understanding of "ornamentation". Their vision being what it was, it is not hard to imagine that they might have envisioned the bleak, unadorned buildings as blank canvases for the future of a dynamic, vibrant neighborhood built benevolently from the ground up by the masters of the city.

Unfortunately, their vision was not only based on false assumptions, namely that the neighborhood did not already have a vibrant community and that it needed the city's urban planners to produce one from scratch, but the plans also neglected a critical element of what kept East Harlem alive — the local businesses. As Rodriguez explains:

> In its need to play Good Samaritan, the city fathers had approved a plan that was the economic death-knell of the neighborhood and similar, New York neighborhoods. Wishing to utilize the entire square footage for apartments, they built city projects that provided no commercial space. Gone were the mom and pop stores that constituted the economic infra-structure of the neighborhood. The candy store, the barber shop, the bodega, the meat market, the cuchifrito stand, the Army & Navy Store — where mom marched us each August to get new pants because we had outgrown our clothing — all gone, disappeared. In place of the ornate turn-of-the-century architecture of the tenements and brownstones, we now had the garish, red, angular brick of the projects. (Rodriguez 1994, pp. 13-14)

With the projects, Rodriguez argues, came the cessation of city services that had supported a community of immigrants struggling to make their own small, enclosed world better. Because the urban planners had left no room for businesses in their master vision of the neighborhood, all commercial activity in the community ceased. The aftermath of the massive closure of all commerce in the neighborhood was devastating:

> As was the case in other parts of the city, when business disappeared from El Barrio, so did the tax base. In each case, however, there was an affluent, mostly white community nearby, where the residents now shopped. For El Barrio, it was Yorkville. The tax dollars which once showed up in the city tax rolls were now showing up in other communities. El Barrio had fewer tax dollars spent so therefore less services: less for education, recreation, sanitation, police, street repairs, and other matters needed to sustain an urban neighborhood. (Rodriguez 1994, p. 14)

The neighborhood fell into disrepair and as the local landowners could no longer afford to maintain the older tenement houses, those too fell victim to the downward spiral of East Harlem.

Had the housing projects themselves lived up to their designers' plans, perhaps Rodriguez, and the others of East Harlem who grew up in their shadow, would have less damning words to say of them. They have succeeded in only one purpose: that of providing affordable housing to residents of the area. The rent-stabilized apartments within the projects are a refuge to families who seek decent housing at affordable prices in one of the most expensive cities in America. José, another of Sharman's profiles, has lived in such housing since it began to appear in East Harlem and "sees buildings like DeWitt Clinton as the only impediment to rampant escalations in the cost of living" (Sharman 2006, p. 76). He is absolutely correct; the buildings' presence, so long as they remain poorly maintained and subsidized, is the greatest deterrent for future investments in East Harlem by wealthier developers and businesses. They are the main reason why the neighborhood did not follow the trajectory of other immigrant neighborhoods in Manhattan, such as Soho, which are now some of the most luxurious residential areas in the entire country.

José's fears of rising housing prices are justified. The prices of non-rent-stabilized apartments, such as the ones my father owns and rents to Sharman and his wife, among others, have been steadily rising thanks to an unrelenting demand from the influx of new, wealthier renters. Even the projects themselves are quickly losing their status as safe havens for affordable housing. One large development, 1199 Plaza, recently turned into a hybrid combination of a rent-stabilized housing project and private co-op building. Eventually, the whole development will be privately owned. The choice for 1199 Plaza to be transferred to the private sector is obvious: of the hideously massive projects in East Harlem, it is the one notable exception. It is also one of two projects I have called home in East Harlem, the other being the Franklin Plaza complex mentioned earlier in this article. The 1199 Plaza development runs from East 108th Street to East 112th Street on First Avenue. Touted as "the city's finest public housing", 1199 Plaza holds some of the best designed apartments ever seen in public housing. Most other housing projects maximize interior space and effectively ignore any sense of interior proportion, thus producing apartments that are dreary, dark, cramped, and functional at best. The buildings of 1199 Plaza, though emulating other projects' lack of ornamentation, defy the box-like structure of other developments. The buildings are "stepped" and "U-shaped", and surround an enormous private playground adjacent to the East River, exclusive and accessible only to the residents of the Plaza via access doors from inside the building.[3] The buildings are also guarded 24 hours a day and it is the only project that has doormen, much like the more exclusive apartment buildings elsewhere in Manhattan. Finally, the entire development is a tribute to the New York skyline. The stepped outlines provide a "variegated skyline" that "resembles a miniaturized version of one of the commonly recognized symbols for the city itself" (Daniels 1983).

Today, 1199 Plaza represents the forces of migration in East Harlem. Because of its architectural separation from other housing projects in the area, it has attracted the attention of private developers and middle-class families alike. Interestingly, many of these families are also ones that moved out of East Harlem years ago to escape escalating crime and violence, but they are slowly coming back as the neighborhood of their childhood is an increasingly more hospitable place to live. The residents of 1199 Plaza still under the US Department of Housing and Urban Development (HUD) jurisdiction are slowly moving out, not because of drastic rent increases but because as they become more upwardly mobile, they seek out even better locations elsewhere. Some, like my family, chose to remain in the neighborhood because of the possibility of ownership of part of the new housing developments, which I will discuss later. Still other residents who are leaving 1199 Plaza are doing so because of natural causes; the elderly are the least susceptible to rent increases because of their unvarying sources of income and thus refuse to leave, but they are also the most susceptible to death.

What you have, then, within just one four-block section of East Harlem, are multiple sources of migration into and out of East Harlem. Immigrant groups continue to come to East Harlem to look for affordable housing at the same time as more affluent groups. Many of the more established groups who settled in the area earlier and have since increased their own economic standing have moved out, as signaled by the steady decline of Puerto Ricans in the area. Thus, migration into East Harlem continues to echo the past, when European immigrants first moved into the area because of its affordable housing and then eventually left as they advanced economically and socially. The anomaly of the current migration patterns, however, is twofold. First, there are competing groups looking for a home in East Harlem, groups with vastly different expectations of what kind of community East Harlem should become. Unlike previous decades, when generally economically homogenous groups (mostly poor) moved into the area, today poor immigrants, middle-class families, and upper-middle-class professionals alike compete with one another for housing. The other difference is that whereas in the past, groups tended to leave East Harlem *en masse*, leaving behind only vestigial reminders of their presence, such as a library, a famous Italian restaurant,

---

3. See 'The List', *The City Review.com*, http://www.thecityreview.com/midbest.htm

or a lone elderly man watching over his block, many of the families who settled earlier in East Harlem and have since accumulated more economic standing are either moving back into the area or are choosing to stay. Because the entire neighborhood is increasingly dynamic, many families, like mine, have invested in the area, recognizing the enormous potential of being an early pioneer in the economic revival of East Harlem. Sadly, however, the good fortune that many of us have experienced has been absent from much of the rest of our neighbors and, as a result, most of the residents who continue to live in East Harlem do so not by choice but because they simply cannot afford to live anywhere else. These competing patterns of migration and settlement suggest that East Harlem is the locus for a unique dynamics of urban political life. The simultaneous demographic change and stagnation means a maximization of interactions between groups in a way that echoes Sassen's call for empowerment "vis-à-vis each other".

Also, 1199 Plaza physically represents these changes. Before the buildings began converting into co-ops, the public spaces of the buildings, like those of many other projects in the area, were often dangerous and disgusting places all at once. Sharman follows José as he rides in an elevator where someone has relieved himself and notes that José and his fellow passengers are experts at navigating around the urine (Sharman 2006, p. 72). Such expertise is common among the residents of East Harlem; I myself have it because of years spent engaged in the same navigational dance in the elevators, staircases, and hallways of 1199 Plaza. Rodriguez's piece, *The Business, 1987*, depicts the illicit sale of drugs inside a typical public stairwell. Though he does not state in what building the stairwell is, I recognize the dark, dimly lit, yet somehow cavernous cement space as the kind one only finds in housing projects. For all its positive elements, 1199 Plaza houses such staircases alongside its amazing apartments. The space is enclosed by cement walls and most likely adorned with only the visible fluorescent light and cement stairs. Its jail-like appearance suggests perhaps the encasing of such illicit activities, as if their obvious presence might somehow be ignored once hidden behind the cement structures. It is almost as if the building designers somehow knew their projects would destroy the neighborhood, wreck its businesses, and drive away the sources of taxation that would provide and sustain viable law enforcement and good schools. After all, the vicious descent of East Harlem in the 1980s, as local law enforcement and the neighborhood alike were unable to stem the flood of crack cocaine, was in large part a direct result of the housing projects (Sharman 2006, p. 97). To hide their guilt, the urban planners built prison-cell staircases where the activities could go on, but at least partially hidden. Because these staircases connect the upper floors of all housing projects to the street, they have essentially provided an unhindered path for New York's underbelly to crawl into the semi-private spaces of homes in the ghetto. For many East Harlemites, these staircases, and the participants of *the business* within them, are the diseases of the neighborhood; evidence of a community entrapped by its very design, which it had no part in planning in the first place.

By the time my father moved our family into La Esperanza Homes, a privately developed and built row of neat town houses on East 112th Street, the staircases, in 1199 Plaza at least, had already been cleaned up. The 1199 Plaza development had already become 1199 Plaza/East River Landing, signifying its hybrid status. The developers of La Esperanza wanted to take the neighborhood's rebirth one step further. Unlike the housing projects of the twentieth century, La Esperanza Homes represents an entirely new attempt at urban planning. Instead of monolithic beasts looming in the skyline, developments such as La Esperanza are low-rise multi-family homes priced for medium-income families. The idea was to lure in middle-class families with the prospect of private ownership; families with a vested interest not just in maximizing property value in the area but also in the community as a whole. Within the ownership contracts, all new owners of La Esperanza Homes are obligated to remain residents in their new homes; such obligations deterred wealthier buyers simply interested in acquiring new property (Sharman 2006, p. 182). The city designed its rules of ownership of La Esperanza to attract families looking for permanent homes of their own. Urban planners felt that respectable middle-class families, such as mine, would leap at the chance to own their piece of the American dream and, in exchange, slowly alter the socio-economic composition of the neighborhood. They were right. La Esperanza Homes was a fantastic success.

The homes themselves are nothing like the high-rise monstrosities dotting the East Harlem skyline. Green cornice moldings contrast against the red-brick facades. The red bricks themselves are slightly lighter than the other red-brick facades around the neighborhood; these are slightly pink in tone. All windows and doors are set underneath white pediments, adding yet another touch of contrast interest to the facade. The pediments themselves are of the plainest kind but their bright white sets off the windows nicely, making the already well-proportioned windows appear even larger. The window frames are all green. Sloping down from the second story main entry is a simple green cement staircase. A green gate separates each home from its neighbor and from the street. All homes have private driveways and garages, an unheard-of luxury in Manhattan. Another rare, and usually expensive, luxury is the private garden each home has in the backyard, accessed by a spiral staircase from a small patio off the combination family room and dining room. The overall effect is that of a row of neatly arranged, precise, symmetrical homes, with enough color contrast and architectural details to remain pleasant to the eye but not ostentatious or gaudy. The designers targeted family-oriented buyers looking for peace and order in a tumultuous world (and tumultuous neighborhood) and La Esperanza Homes, at first glance, offers just that.

When the families first moved into La Esperanza Homes, each home was exactly the same. Now, almost seven years after the first family moved in, each house is beginning to take on its own personality. Within one single block of homes — East 112th Street between Second and Third Avenues — reside families of every ethnic background, each with unique ideas on aesthetics, landscaping, and interior design. Here, in just one block, is the future of East Harlem — its racial politics subtly delineated by the gentle pronouncements of individual identities alongside equally subtle, but poignant, cases of identity fluidity. My family owns and lives in one of these homes. Our neighbors are Caucasian American, Puerto Rican, Mexican, Japanese, Chinese, Italian (recently emigrated from Italy), Dominican, and black American. The owners of the home to the immediate left of mine keep Christmas lights on their staircase all year round. They are a country family, proud of their roots in rural America, and a complex mix of ethnic and racial backgrounds. They keep mostly to themselves, although one of their children, a medical student who worked as a nurse overseas in China, regularly converses with my parents to practice his Chinese. Naturally, their idea of the simpler life also directly conflicts with my father's approach to garden aesthetics. Our neighbors have taken the simpler approach to gardening: seven years ago they planted one rose plant, installed one bench to sit on, and have not touched the garden since. Their weeds and rose plant grow unchecked and, in a fitting tribute to Salvatore Rosa, have grown so tall that they cast long, dark shadows over the entire garden. My father, on the other hand, a former engineer, loathes unruliness and disorder. His idea of a proper garden consists of neatly-arranged parallel rows of flowering shrubs, a well-trimmed and groomed vegetable patch, and a tiered row of trees, medium-height shrubs, and ground-cover plants, all of which surround a precisely-laid brick courtyard with a water feature as the centerpiece.

The sources of differing aesthetic tastes do not simply end with the differences between rural and urban. One family proudly displays a lovely nativity scene in their driveway all year round. Their front entryway, always visible since the family likes to keep the front door to their home open to the street, houses a picture of the Madonna and a traditional Chinese wall decoration symbolizing good fortune. The matriarch of the family also happens to love Chinese art and decor. The wall hanging was a Christmas gift from my parents. They have many more different Chinese decorations throughout their house — all either gifts from my family or purchased curios from Chinatown. The eclectic blend of religious and secular art, Chinese and Hispanic, antique and kitsch is the product of a family's simultaneous pride in who they are and open-minded aesthetic tastes. The nativity scene is not offensive, nor is it intrusive to non-Catholic pedestrians walking by their home. It is a loving tribute to the birth of a religious figure who the family believes guides them morally, ethically, and spiritually every day. The contrasting Chinese pieces are a testament to their bond with their neighbors; neighbors who they might never have met had the city not re-evaluated its urban planning schema for East Harlem. In a way, fortune plays a critical role in the changes of East Harlem, and though the wall hanging wishes good fortune to that family, it is as if through their perennially open front door, good fortune might also visit all of East Harlem.

That family also has stone Chinese lions guarding their driveway, a design feature they installed after watching my father put in a pair of antique stone lions on our driveway. Theirs were purchased from a landscaping company in New York. Ours, on the other hand, were carefully selected by my father on one of our trips to China and shipped here. The defining features of our driveway are those lions, bamboo plantings, evergreen trees flanking the garage door, and our immaculately tiled staircase, the first on the block. Sharman (2006, p. 162) comments rather humorously that virtually every architectural feature unique to the Pan home is a "homage to the nearest home improvement store". This, too, is a reflection of my parents' background; my father was an engineer in a shipyard that built warships for the Chinese navy and my mother's love of cleanliness and hyperorganization comes from her days as a nursery school teacher and her own mother's compulsive cleaning habits. The hand-carved statues, along with framed silk napkins embroidered with delicate, traditional Chinese designs and several large Chinese paintings in the living room, all clearly visible from the street, are symptomatic of my family's determination to be at once a part of and distinct from the community. Sharman (2006, p. 19) writes of my father: "In telling Si Zhi's story, I explore how he and others like him maintain a sense of community that reaffirms transnational ties without abdicating a connection to their host country." My father's ability to navigate between the community of East Harlem and our roots in Shanghai is not unlike what the nativity scene down the street represents. In a way, these separate declarations of identity are the individual cogs in a larger East Harlem dynamic; each piece separate yet inextricably interconnected with the next, together creating momentum to launch East Harlem into its next historical epoch.

New York City is notorious for offering residential areas so closely spaced that residents can often tell what their neighbors are having for dinner. More important than their meal selections, perhaps, are the varying tastes in art displayed on the walls. Because of the sheer impossibility of absolute privacy in as tight a space as New York City, private tastes become immediately visible and obvious to the larger public. Just as "dwellings are the basic, repeated units in an urban neighborhood", so do the interiors of private homes in East Harlem, often visible from street level, reflect microcosmically many of the political dynamics of shared experience in greater East Harlem (Hayden 1995, p. 34). Were you to step out into the row of side-by-side backyards behind La Esperanza Homes, you might notice, through the oversized windows that mark dining and family rooms, two of the homes sporting Asian ink-style paintings with a distinctly modern touch. One is my house and the other is the two-bedroom apartment of one of our neighbors in the house to our right. His work, renowned in Taiwan and Japan, has just recently been featured in art galleries around New York and he is quickly gaining notice for his brilliant fusion of Chinese- and Japanese-style ink paintings with contemporary art. The transition from ancient to modern, Eastern to Western, however, is completely fluid, and his paintings alone reflect the marriage of East Asian and Western cultures that comes with increasing economic interdependence.

Sadly, real life does not reflect as flawless a marriage of cultures as my neighbor's paintings might suggest. The young son of our Japanese neighbors was turned away from the neighborhood public school for suspiciously ambiguous reasons. After a good deal of arguing, cajoling, and threatening of lawsuits, the school finally accepted the boy. His younger sister now attends the school as well. The school's reluctance to accept this young child because of his ethnic background is no surprise. Recall Pete's earlier admonition against letting the Chinese come into the neighborhood. East Harlem and its residents must reckon daily with the forces of change that are constantly altering the neighborhood's social, economic, and racial demographics. Experiments in urban planning such as La Esperanza have brought in greater ethnic diversity, heightening racial tensions, which have at times become violent.[4] Despite the sporadic violence, the tension is "less about outright prejudice than it is a reflection of the bitterness many ... feel about losing their cultural and economic dominance in the community" (Sharman 2006, p. 46). Unfortunately for those who have trouble accepting these changes, these demographic and power shifts are only likely to increase as East Harlem, alongside the new "Harlem renaissance", marches steadily onward. The economic changes are even more drastic, simply because they are occurring much faster than anyone could have anticipated. New businesses are beginning to appear throughout the neighborhood, catering to both the traditional working-class immigrant community and also to the new influx of middle- and upper-income families and singles. Unlike the collapse of the commercial sector following the build-up of the massive housing projects in the 1960s and 1970s, contemporary development in the area includes large tracts of commercial space for future businesses. Camilo José Vergara memorialized the former Corn Exchange Bank on East 125th Street and Park Avenue in his book *American Ruins*. At the time Vergara's book came out in 1999, the building had deteriorated so far that he writes: "I thought that in choosing this setting I would not need to explain what I meant by ruins" (1999, p. 88). The abandoned building maintains its original Romanesque Revival and Queen Anne features, and its grand scale and ornate detailing remind us of a time when East Harlem was a thriving community with a vibrant commercial base (Vergara 1999, p. 88). Left to deteriorate for over 20 years, the building was the perfect symbol of the demise of East Harlem into irretrievable ghetto status. Despite its past degradation, today, even the Corn Exchange Bank faces a likely facelift and new life: it is scheduled to become a "mixed-use site" for the Harlem Culinary Institute and 12,600 square feet of commercial space (Stoler, 2006).[5] In the residential sector, the success of La Esperanza has paved the way for more private real estate development in the

---

4. *West Side Story* describes the tension between Puerto Ricans and Italians in the 1950s. In perhaps another twist of fate, and an example of the ways in which lifeworlds collide, Bernstein's two darling granddaughters are lower school students at the Brearley School, where I attended middle and upper school. I babysat for the girls many times and it is ironic that I should be writing about the same racial tensions their grandfather wrote about almost 60 years ago. Gang wars along racial lines have always occurred in East Harlem, particularly as one ethnic group threatened to replace another. Italians, Puerto Ricans, Mexicans, blacks, and others have all, at one time or another, fought each other. Gang wars between different Hispanic nationalities still exist. On a less organized level, racially motivated crimes still occur all too often. These incidents, however, are increasingly few and far between, and the kind gestures such as the open-armed embrace of our neighbors of my family as fellow East Harlemites suggest that they are quickly becoming the exception rather than the norm.

5. See also 'Neighborhood Sites and Landmarks', *East Harlem Preservation*, http://www.eastharlempreservation.org/docs/landmarks.htm

neighborhood. Dawnay, Day, a London-based investment bank, has recently invested over US$200 million in East Harlem. As one executive told the media:

> East Harlem is the last area of the whole of Manhattan being gentrified. This is the area close to Mount Sinai Hospital — you go down the streets and there are a lot of shopping centres being opened up. There are lots of young professionals moving in. It is a bit like buying in Brixton 15 years ago, where house prices have since gone up fivefold. (Rossiter 2007)

Though Dawnay, Day has yet to begin developing its new properties, one new building hints at the future of East Harlem. At the very northwest corner of East Harlem, sitting on a single block where East Harlem has ended but Central Park has not yet begun, 111 Central Park North recently set a record for the most expensive condo sold in Harlem, a frightening US$6.6 million.[6] Dawnay, Day's comparison of East Harlem to Brixton is a misguided one; East Harlem's prices are nearing the five-fold increase of Brixton, but completing the feat in seven years, not fifteen.[7] The arrival of international firms such as Dawnay, Day and the daily struggles of disenfranchised groups, such as my father and neighbors' fight to send their children to school, are truly testaments to Sassen's (2003, p. 26) declaration that "the large city of today, especially the global city, emerges as a strategic site for ... global corporate capital ... but ... also where the formation of new claims by informal political actors materializes and assumes concrete form".

The response to such growth is mixed. Just about everyone agrees that the changes have brought in increased public services, most notably an increase in police efficacy and thus lower crime rates (Garland 2003). What most differ on is whether these increased public services are worth their cost. Some, such as owners of La Esperanza Homes and many other similar developments throughout the neighborhood, welcome the increase in their home values. Others protest against the certain rise in rent as the neighborhood becomes increasingly gentrified (Associated Press 2007).[8] Still others have been protesting that the developments

---

6. See 'Records Set in 2006', *111 Central Park North*, http://www.111centralparknorth.com/media/news/newsRecords2006.pdf
7. Sharman reports that five years after the sale of the La Esperanza homes, similar new developments in East Harlem were sold at $750 000, compared with the $340 900 price tag on La Esperanza. Sharman himself attended a community information meeting where the developers tried to explain the rationale for the prohibitively high cost of these homes. Asked to explain how low- and middle-income families in East Harlem could be expected to generate such high monthly mortgage payments for these new homes which were nearly identical to the La Esperanza projects, the developers suggested that buyers could make a down-payment of $100 000 to offset costs later. Sharman writes that several audience members laughed out loud at the suggestion (Sharman 2006, p. 202). I suspect that Sharman himself was probably chuckling quietly in disbelief. These events took place in 2005. Today, market values for La Esperanza homes are somewhere between $1 million and $1.5 million. While the lucky homeowners of La Esperanza are rejoicing in these sky-rocketing values, there remains little hope for other East Harlemites who wish to capture a share of their own American dream.
8. For an excellent example of community outrage against real estate developers and rising housing costs, see José Rivera's 28 August 2005 post on the community updates page of his website on the East Harlem community: http://www.east-harlem.com/mt/archives/cat_community_news.html

take over cherished public community spaces, such as Green Thumb community gardens.[9]

The competing voices have taken shape in many forms in the area, including the manifestation of increasingly political street art. James De La Vega, a long-time Puerto Rican resident of East Harlem and one of the most prolific street artists in New York City, has drawn multiple murals protesting against the gentrification of East Harlem. One drawing, a simple chalk statement scrawled on a wall, declares: "Don't think for a minute that we haven't noticed that the 96th St. boundary has moved further North." De La Vega's art is an example of what Hayden describes as public art:

> Scale and cost are not the defining elements of a public, urban language. Rather, it is a metaphorical ingenuity that enables the creators of some projects to summon the resonance of public urban life, while others fail and their projects fall flat. (Hayden 1995, p. 75)

De La Vega's work goes beyond simple, but powerful, chalk messages. His work revolves around themes central to East Harlem, from political messages regarding gentrification to religiously themed murals, and massive memorials to notable figures in the community. Perhaps paradoxically to his overtly political messages, most of De La Vega's work reflects the growing optimism of the neighborhood that has come about since the area's rebirth. He often leaves inspiring messages to the members of the area on sidewalks, encouraging the young to dream and advocating peace and harmony. His is a project that truly reflects not only his Puerto Rican roots but those of the entire neighborhood. His messages inspire not just the Puerto Rican youth but all the young residents of East Harlem. In a way, all of the inhabitants, even the wealthy young professionals, have moved to East Harlem looking for new opportunities, be they cheap rent, economic growth, citizenship, or the great American dream. When Sassen (2003, p. 16) explains that "global cities make possible the emergence of new types of political subjects arising out of conditions of acute disadvantage", the residents of East Harlem fit her description perfectly. We have all come from acute disadvantage. Indeed, even the wealthy professionals who have moved to East Harlem have done so because, while they are wealthy compared to their new neighbors, they have been pushed out of other areas in Manhattan precisely because, in the most expensive city in the country, "wealthy" is a very relative term.

East Harlem is changing rapidly. As its social composition shifts, just like it did in the 1950s when the Puerto Ricans first arrived in the area, and the late 1800s before that when the Italians began moving in, the residents must contend with a shift in power structures as settled groups become displaced by new arrivals. The demographics of the neighborhood are changing. New businesses are opening and new homes are built and sold every day, bringing exponential increases in the cost of living. These changes, like any major demographic shift in an

---

9. See 'Gardeners, Developers, Police in Standoff in Harlem', *On NY Turf*, 3 April 2007, http://www.onnyturf.com/articles/read.php?article_id=519

area, have their advantages and disadvantages, depending on one's perspective. The increased presence of wealthier inhabitants and a higher tax base has provided more public services, including better law enforcement.[10] Crime rates have plummeted as drastically as they skyrocketed in the 1980s. But the threat of rising costs of living also terrifies many residents as they fear being pushed out of a neighborhood they have inhabited for decades, perhaps generations. These changes are all indicated by the gradual replacement of the ruined tenement buildings and gigantic public housing projects with new, privately owned developments. The changes in the structural outline of the neighborhood reflect the demographic shifts — old giving way to new.

Despite some resistance, most of the veteran East Harlem residents accept the changes happening around them. Now we see not just traditional Puerto Rican symbols or religious emblems but a medley of all the different symbols reflecting the diversity of the residents of the area. Each home is unique, but shared details, such as a love of Chinese accessories or a fondness for roses in the backyard, suggest the subtle ways in which all the separate identities have come together into a larger East Harlem community. Out of this new, hybrid East Harlem community rises a new class of political subjects; cosmopolitan residents of a global enclave within a global city, each personally invested in the future of East Harlem, New York, the world. The very existence of this hybridized community calls into question traditional lines of distinction within urban life — poor versus rich, white versus black, powerful versus weak. Perhaps that is what Homi Bhabha (2006, p. 162) envisioned when he explained the power of the hybridized symbols of authority: "Hybridity intervenes in the exercise of authority not merely to indicate the impossibility of its identity but to represent the unpredictability of its presence". If East Harlem is indeed the post-colonial city of Sassen's imagining, the traditional power structures of New York have been disrupted by the constantly evolving dynamics of one of its most underrated and ignored neighborhoods.

After all, for all the changes in East Harlem over the last 200 years, the residents today are still just like the immigrants who first settled in the neighborhood in the early 1800s. Living in what is still one of the poorest neighborhoods in New York, even if it is rapidly becoming not so, we are all aspiring, dreaming, working for a better life for ourselves and our children. Our shared dreams of something better are more powerful forces of change than any larger corporate or statist ones. It was our dreams that brought us together to East Harlem, Spanish Harlem, El Barrio. And together we are creating a dynamic new community, full of pride, strength, activism, and power. Our place, East Harlem, and

---

10. Some might argue that law enforcement is more effective because whites are moving into the neighborhood. I would argue otherwise — the rates were steadily dropping well before the noticeable appearance of white residents largely because by the mid to late 1990s, the city had already begun to evaluate East Harlem as a potential source for new development. Money, I would argue, played a much bigger role in bringing in both wealthy whites and better law enforcement. Whichever way you look at it, crime has dropped and that has benefited everyone in the neighborhood, except perhaps the criminals.

our community have lived up to Jordan's (2003, p. 31) assertion that both "have the potential to persist — and to emerge in new configurations". After decades of decline, East Harlem and its diverse patchwork of citizens have re-emerged as not just a neighborhood, but as a home.

References

Associated Press (2007) 'Real Estate Firm Draws Protests in Harlem', *The New York Sun*, 4 April, http://www.nysun.com/article/51804.
Bhabha, H. (2006) *The Location of Culture*, Routledge, New York.
Clemence, S. (2005) 'Most Expensive Zip Codes 2005', *Forbes.com*, 26 April, http://www.forbes.com/2005/04/26/cx_sc_0426home.html.
Daniels, L. A. (1983) 'About Real Estate; Exhibit on Growth of New York as a City of Renters', *The New York Times*, 15 July, http://query.nytimes.com/gst/fullpage.html?res=9A05E5DA1539F936A25754C0A965948260&sec=&spon=&pagewanted=1.
Garland, S. E. (2003) 'Operation Impact', *East Harlem News*, 1 May, http://www.east-harlem.com/mt/archives/cat_community_news.html.
Hayden, D. (1995) *The Power of Place: Urban Landscapes as Public History*, The MIT Press, Cambridge, MA.
Jordan, J. (2003) 'Collective Memory and Locality in Global Cities', in Krause, L. & Petro, P. (eds), *Global Cities: Cinema, Architecture, and Urbanism in a Digital Age*, Rutgers University Press, New Brunswick, NJ.
Kincaid, J. (1999) *My Garden Book*, Farrar, Straus and Giroux, New York.
Kittler, F. (2006) 'The City Is a Medium', *Excerpter*, 2 October, http://excerpter.wordpress.com/2006/10/02/friedrich-kittler-the-city-is-a-medium/.
Rancière, J. (2006) 'The Politics of Aesthetics', *16Beaver*, http://www.16beavergroup.org/mtarchive/archives/001877.php.
Rodriguez, J. (1994) *American Scene: Spanish Harlem*, National Museum of American Art, Washington, DC.
Rossiter, J. (2007) 'Dawnay, Day Bets £250m on Harlem Makeover', *Times Online*, 26 March, http://business.timesonline.co.uk/tol/business/industry_sectors/banking_and_finance/article1567272.ece.
Rybczynski, W. (1986) *Home: A Short History of an Idea*, Viking, New York.
Sassen, S. (2003) 'Reading the City in a Global Digital Age', in Krause, L. & Petro, P. (eds), *Global Cities: Cinema, Architecture, and Urbanism in a Digital Age*, Rutgers University Press, New Brunswick, NJ.
Sharman, R. (2006) *The Tenants of East Harlem*, University of California Press, Berkeley, CA.
Stoler, M. (2006) 'Harlem Staging Its Latest Renaissance', *The New York Sun*, 14 September, http://www.nysun.com/article/39643?page_no=1.
Vergara, C. J. (1999) *American Ruins*, Monacelli Press, New York.

Genre and the African City: The Politics and Poetics of Urban Rhythms

Sam Okoth Opondo

This article engages the genre—city intertext in order to make conceptual distinctions between the "city" and the "urban" by illustrating how certain textual representations and disciplinary practices in their constitution of the African city are actively involved in the killing of the plurality of rhythms, or heterogeneity central to urban life. It illustrates how certain modes of reading and writing about the African city (colonial autobiographies, Eurocentric ethnographies) and institutionalized forms of non-contamination or non-contradiction (nation-building practices, museums and colonial or post-colonial urban planning) in their attempt to uphold a generic image of Africanness or citiness are constitutive of rhythmic urbicide — the killing of urban heterogeneity through claims to purity and partitioning of African cities, subjects and subject voices.

The City is a discourse and this discourse is truly a language: the city speaks to its inhabitants, we speak our city, the city where we are, simply by living in it, by wandering through it, by looking at it. (Barthes 1997)

African writers ... are [by ethnicity] Asante, Yoruba, Kikuyu, but what does this now mean? They are [by nationality] Ghanaian, Nigerian, Kenyan, but does this yet mean anything? They are [by racial identification] black, and what is the worth of the black person? ... This particular constellation of problems is not often found outside Africa: a recent colonial history, a multiplicity of diverse sub national indigenous traditions, a foreign language whose metropolitan culture has traditionally defined the "natives" by race as inferior. (Appiah 1993)

Out of Africa: Autobiography as Ethnogeography

"I had a farm in Africa at the foot of the Ngong Hills." This is the oft-cited opening line of Karen Blixen's (Isak Dinesen's) memoir *Out of Africa* (1937). Structured as a collage of characters and experiences that merge to form Blixen's memories of Africa — its landscape, rhythms and cultures — the text presents Africa as a pastoral landscape in which men exist in a truer form than they do in Europe. Beginning with an idyllic description of everyday life on the African farm where colonial settlers, African "natives" and wild animals live in harmony, Blixen introduces us to her Kikuyu cook Kamante and a domesticated bushbuck Lulu, and uses these two to illustrate the connection of her farm to the native community and the African landscape. For example, Lulu the bushbuck is said to make "the house one with the African landscape, so that nobody could tell where the one stopped and the other began" (Dinesen 1992, p. 80), while at the same time providing a rhythmic basis for dealing with or coming to terms with the African native. As Blixen aptly points out:

> When you have caught the rhythm of Africa, you find that it is the same in all her music. What I learnt from the game of the country was useful to me in my dealings with Africans. (Blixen 1984, p. 24)

In positing such a uniform rhythm, Blixen, in her affection for the natives, rugged nature and animals, resorts to forms of imagery, motifs and symbols that privilege a pastoral aesthetic which erases the plurality of African modes of meaning-making by equating them with nature. The violence of such rhetorical gestures is well captured in Ngugi wa Thiong'o's reading of Blixen's *Out of Africa* as a work that metaphorically merges African topography with human anatomy in a manner that excludes the social and political conditions of African existence. According to Thiong'o (1981, p. 19), Blixen invokes a hierarchical "cosmic picture" which features Africans only to the extent that they form "parts of wood and stones" and marks them as different "only because they occasionally exhibit impulses towards animals".

Read with the appropriate discernment, *Out of Africa* emerges as an account of European possession, reinvention and representation of African lands, peoples and cultures. As illustrated by Thiong'o, Blixen engages in a literary invention of a pristine Africa by exploiting the tropes of nature and purity, thus naturalizing her possession of the farm while erasing the violence of colonial occupation. She downplays the political economy of settler colonialism in Kenya and presents the African farm, complete with its squatting native population and wildlife, as the place where she "ought to be" (Blixen 1984, p. 1). In so doing, Blixen repartitions the British East African colony along a country—city dichotomy with the city being a place of whiteness, decadence and middle-class adventurism.

It is not overstating the case to assert that *Out of Africa* provides an appropriate starting point for an exploration of the politics of genre and the African city. The nostalgic pastoral genre that it articulates must not be read as a country story in exclusion of the city or the political and social formations that make it possible. It is better read alongside or against those other narratives which challenge the aspects of intelligibility that it tries to preserve. Unless we are attentive to the politics of genre, narratives of the type that *Out of Africa* represents will continue to teach us what they have always taught us: to forget the other side of the story; to see an Africa caught up in perpetual rurality and accessible only through sites and reading practices that silence the various voices and positioned utterances through which meanings in everyday life are mediated. For Blixen, the authentic African is situated "allochronically" (see Fabian 1983, p. 155) in relationship to the European. That is, African modes of life are put in another time, associated with either earlier periods of individual life (childhood) or of human history (primitivism), thus advocating their exclusion from modern or urban forms of life and denying the coeval emergence of these two ways of being.

It is worthwhile to note that Karen Blixen's literary canonization proliferates a textually invented Africa that assigns African places and people an inherent aesthetic value, thus setting them apart as material for the exotic, the grotesque or the bizarre. This reflects a colonial racial—spatial order that manifests itself in settler expansionism and safari intrusion, which continues to haunt the political imaginary of post-colonial Nairobi.

The problematic character of such approaches to Africa are at the centre of V. Y. Mudimbe's *The Invention of Africa* (1988), an elaborate interrogation of the construction of Africa through Eurocentric categories and conceptual systems, from anthropology and missionary discourses to philosophy (the problem of gnosis and the colonial library). Within such a figuration, knowledge about Africa, even when produced by Africans themselves, is usually in furtherance of an alterity conceived of and developed by Europeans.

Today, essentially the same gesture, if in reverse, is made by the planners of the affluent *Mzungu*-dominated (European-dominated) Karen suburb in Nairobi, which sits on part of what was Karen Blixen's farm. Within policy circles, the suburb's racial and colonial history is overcoded by planning practices that foreground a rhetoric of "threat" which fails to problematize the socio-economic and historical contexts within which such threats emerge. For example, the *Karengata [Karen and Langata] Local Physical Development Plan 2005-2015* (LPDP) (Ministry of Lands and Housing, Physical Planning Department & City Council of Nairobi, City Planning Department 2005) attempts to identify the threats and, in the process, constitutes an impoverished, dehistoricized image of Karengata. According to the planners, Karengata,

> [o]nce the most prestigious residential area in Nairobi, is now under threat. The recent surge of unregulated and environmentally damaging development led residents to call for urgent action before the area's living environment suffered irreversible decline.

Among the threats to Karen's prestige and environment identified in the LPDP are the footpaths that serve as access routes for low-income labourers but can also be used as getaway routes for criminals, and kiosks that offer affordable supplies but also serve as hideouts for criminals and contribute to congestion that slows down traffic and compromises the aesthetic appeal of the area. Also mentioned is the Maasai village at Karen Plains by the Mokoyeti River, where 25 families seeking pasture for their cattle during the drought of 1984 settled and now challenge any of the "title holders" who attempt to build in the area. According to the LPDP, the threat can be alleviated through strategic mapping and restructuring of footpaths, and demolition or relocation of kiosks so as to break the polyrhythm created by the proletariat. Similarly, the Maasai who have "taken to demolishing walls and fences ... that threaten their traditional lifestyle are to be forced to adapt to a more urban existence".

In developing a plan that sees the Maasai way of life as a threat to suburban aesthetics and modes of ownership, Karengata residents and planners employ a language and attitude reminiscent of the November 1967 *Maasai Progress Plan* — an attempt by the Tanzanian government to rid the Maasai community of certain cultural practices that were considered ancient, unhealthy and embarrassing or detrimental to the national development goals of Julius Nyerere's *Ujamaa* brand of "African socialism" (Schneider 2006, p. 105). Most notable of these attempts to make the "modern African man", and by extension the "African nation", was Operation Dress-Up, a campaign to induce the Maasai community in Tanzania to abandon their traditional mode of dress and adopt modern clothing like the rest of post-colonial Tanzanians. Within this national imaginary, the Maasai's withdrawal from what was considered "normal" attire was seen as a reversal of the pace of progress occurring among other groups in the country. Thus, the dressing-up of the Maasai was seen as an imperative of nation-building; a disciplinary measure geared towards modernization, provision of equal opportunity and national integration. That is, the Maasai were to be brought into the national time of "African socialism" by being dressed up in European clothes. The spatial character of this discordance of ideas of Africanness is expressed in the disciplinary practice set to prevent members of the nomadic Maasai community from entering the Arusha metropolis while "wearing limited skin clothing or loose blanket", and the government's threat of retribution if they clung to such "awkward clothing" (Mazrui 1970, p. 19).

Sensitivity to the representational codes through which these threats are constituted yields insight into the form of the isolationism that informs Karen's (both Blixen and the suburb) social, cultural and moral imaginaries. It invites analysis of the mechanics of representational practices that produce otherness and attempt to discipline heterogeneity through a political apparatus that turns on the recognition and disavowal of racial, cultural and historical differences. It also highlights how this provides an impetus for violence by resisting negotiation through forms that prescribe fidelity to a colonial or bourgeois script while excluding or appropriating local cultures and aesthetics in an assimilative manner. On the whole, this construction of otherness is not an innocent exercise; its objective, whether stated or not, is to construe subject peoples as a population of degenerate types on the basis of their rhythms of life and develop strategies for dealing with them.

The political expediency of such generic representations is best captured through the imaginative geographies that they enable and the material forms in which they are circulated. Following what Gaston Bachelard called a "poetics of space" (Bachelard 1969), Edward Said illustrates how imaginative geographies sustain images that dramatize distance and are productive of identity/alterity. According to Said:

space acquires emotional and even rational sense by a kind of poetic process, whereby vacant or anonymous reaches of distance are converted into meaning for us here. The same process occurs when we deal with time. Much of what we associate with or even know about such periods as "long ago" or even "the beginning" or "at the end of time" is poetic-made up. (Said 1978, p. 55)

Thus, through a cinematic treatment of *Out of Africa*, and the subsequent transformation of the Blixen house into the Karen Blixen Museum, we are now constantly reminded of the colonial perspective of Karen Blixen and the suburb that takes up her name.

Emerging from Sydney Pollack's 1985 cinema adaptation of *Out of Africa* (starring Meryl Streep and Robert Redford) is a redemption of the political and physical reality that exposes the relationship between the Manichean colonial city and modes of spatialization and intelligibility which are complicit in the transformation of the Maasai country into a "farm in Africa at the foot of the Ngong Hills" where the Maasai are seen as being co-extensive with the African landscape, and later on into the Karen suburb where Maasai living in their traditional form are considered a threat to suburban life.

Also arising from the cinema-inspired museumization of the Karen Blixen (Bogani) house is an erasure of the public—private sphere split through processes that recast it as a symbolic part of Nairobi's cultural heritage. Such an institutionalized symbolization of what had been textually represented as private property in Blixen's *Out of Africa* inevitably draws on the cultural assumptions and resources of the people who make it (Lavine & Karp 1991, p. 1). It emphasizes one element of cultural life and downplays others and, in the process, legitimizes forms of consumption that represent a marriage between post-colonial urban capitalism and colonial lineages, where exclusionary tendencies continue to set residents and visitors apart from the centralized "African city".

Perhaps a consideration of the spectral character of Blixen's "African farm" and the different ways in which it haunts the post-colonial Nairobian imaginary can help us mark a genre—city intertext which accords recognition to how the African city is poeticized and to the modes of subjectification that transform individual bodies into a body politic. Such a geo-poetic[1] reading of the African city takes note of the boundaries, divisions and hierarchies (the focus of geography and ethnography) that animate the city, while remaining attentive to the rhythms, transversal practices and micropolitics of everyday life (the geo-poetic and ethno-poetic additions and transgressions). This geo-poetic focus makes it possible to identify and experience those everyday practices that "cut across" or provide alternatives to acts of representation that work to "circumscribe and maintain a particular subjective territory".[2] Looking from a mobile viewpoint,

---

1. The term 'poetics' as used in this article is meant to include different forms of 'self-fashioning' or modes of reconstitution of selves and others through specific exclusions, conventions and discursive practices. More specifically, it is the interplay of imaginative and fictional discourse — plays, poetry (prose, verse, haptic and visual poems), novels and stories (see Shapiro 1985, p. 402; Clifford 1986, p. 24).
2. For a more elaborate explanation of transversal poetics, see Reynolds (2003, p. 4).

the transversal practices of walking, talking, reading and sitting across spaces, genres and cultures can be seen as spatial organizations with a haptic dimension (one connecting bodies and spaces) that redefines relations across race, gender, sexuality and age by providing a different sense of the self, place and other.[3]

Nyarloka's Geo-poetics: Reading the Exilic City

What the map cuts up, the story cuts across. (Certeau 1984, p. 129)

While Blixen's *Out of Africa* revolves around narratives of everyday life in the "African farm" and the romanticizing of authentic Africanness, native inclusion and rurality, a contrapuntal reading of this pastoral story reveals the *double-writing* (see Doty 1996) within the narrative. Such a reading practice problematizes Blixen's occupation of the farm by mapping other places of encounter where identities are constructed and negotiated, and highlights the multiple sites where colonial violence is originated, symbolized and managed in a manner that makes it possible for her to own the farm.

Through such a reading, the urban spaces and processes of African dispossession that create the conditions of possibility for Blixen's coffee farming, literary engagements and idealization of the African pastoral become more apparent. Reading these two stories together goes a long way toward illustrating the epistemic, physical and structural violence of a politics of moralizing predicated upon rooted identities, and prompts us to rethink our conceptions of Africanness and, with that, the African city.

To approach this issue, we must first diversify our sites of analysis in order to read back that which has been put under erasure by a Eurocentric or colonialist politics of representation and the writing practices and genres of expression that favour it. This escape from, or resistance to, forms of cultural governance and representational practices that attempt to install urban or African exclusivity through the disciplining of urban heterogeneity is crucial as it suggests the interrogation and pluralizing of our conceptions of the political by forestalling the demand to secure a "true or pure African identity". With this in mind, African cultures of expression can be understood as complex intersections of multiple places, historical temporalities and subject positions (Mitchell 1995, p. 83). And it is by locating the African city as a form of enunciatory space that it becomes possible for us to identify the forces that are actively involved in the construction of subjects who are co-extensive with the spaces they occupy, and the positionality that they manifest within this space. To illustrate this point, it is important that we consider the poetics and politics of everyday life in urban spaces and what such a consideration suggests for the idea of Africanness.

---

3. The genre—city—body relationship and the gendered character of (e)motion in reading the city are discussed in Bruno (1997). Similar explorations are made by de Certeau in his essay 'Walking in the City', which points out the transversal character of what he calls 'the long poem of walking' that manipulates spatial organizations (Certeau 1984, p. 101).

Andrew Hake's *African Metropolis* (1977) is instructive as a point of departure. Hake outlines the dual character of the urban revolution in Kenya by mapping the simultaneous development of the "modern" city alongside a self-help city that escapes representation (p. 4).

Hake's reading of the self-help city as a world apart from the planned city provides exemplary insight into the echoes and footprints of a colonial past at play in post-colonial Nairobi. Unlike Blixen, Hake historicizes the spatial arrangements of the city and calls our attention to the politically sanctioned geographies that are often taken for granted. For example, we are able to appreciate how parts of Nairobi's built environment, the city's porosity and social infrastructure are a reflection of colonial zoning practices, racial planning and a moral economy based on the South African model[4], or planning experiments such as Ebenezer Howard's "garden city" concept.[5]

In addition, it becomes possible for us to see how urban difference slides from being predominantly racial in the colonial era to a post-colonial setting where class, gender and diverse conceptions of ethnicity are the main markers of difference. It is interesting, therefore, to see how what used to be colonial squatter settlements like Pumwani, Kibera and Mathare are still marginalized as they are transformed to present-day slums that maintain ethnic arrangements which replicate rural ethnoscapes with their attendant inter-ethnic tensions, while African housing estates established in areas like Ofafa, Ziwani, Makadara, Jericho and Maringo continue to be the sites where Nairobi's urban poor live.

While the above reading is useful for mapping the socio-economic and historical basis of certain spheres of urban life in Nairobi, Hake points out that there are as many Nairobis as there are inhabitants. Nairobi as an idea or place emerges as something different for each one of these inhabitants, depending on their position in the city. For Hake, an analysis predicated on socio-economic categories cannot catch the dense atmosphere of city life. In support of an aesthetic idiom in the figuring of the city, Hake suggests an appreciation of various genres of expression and the extent to which they render the city's illegibility legible:

> Perhaps only the novelist can help us know the living experience, only the artist, the songwriter or the film-maker can capture the vivid flashes of light and colour that make mere descriptions so drab. (Hake 1977, p. 10)

This sentiment is shared by J. Roger Kurtz (1998, p. 8), who points out that the post-colonial urban novel "provides insights into the societies that produced

---

4. Post-colonial Nairobi is to a large extent polarized along the lines established during the colonial era. Zoning practices were mainly on the basis of racial segregation recommended by planning commissions (see the Williams Report of 1907 and Feethams Report of 1926). The native housing estates in Nairobi's Eastlands were separated from the white-dominated Westlands by the Indian bazaar.

5. In his *To-morrow: A Peaceful Path to Real Reform* (1898) and *Garden Cities of To-morrow* (1902), Ebenezer Howard lays out his conception of the 'garden city', a town that combines the best of both worlds, of the city and the landscape. Behind this new concept of the garden city, Howard saw a recipe for urban problems and rural ills based on managed urban population, the creation of a green belt and other means of making the city sustainable.

them". The novel presents us with multiple "small cities"[6] such that the cityscape can be identified not only by what it reveals but also by what it conceals. It also exposes the gaps that face the city dweller and the multiple acts of invention – the *poesis* that makes up everyday life. The multiple voices that make up the novel also constitute a narrative cartography that presents "urban life as a landscape of partial visibilities and manifold possibilities that exclude in the very act of inviting" with the net effect of "inaccessibility being different with each city dweller, according to the nature of his/her outsiderness" (Wirth-Nesher 1996, p. 9).

A clue to this partial and fragmentary character of the city is provided in the poetry of Marjorie Oludhe Macgoye. Like Blixen, Oludhe Macgoye maps Africa from an unusual position. She is a white woman married to a Kenyan Luo man. Being attentive to her locus of enunciation, she resists the naturalizing tendencies that make Blixen talk of Africa as the "place where I ought to be". In contrast, Oludhe Macgoye positions herself as Nyarloka (the Dholuo term for a "foreign daughter") and uses this ironic distance to read the city in a manner that allows her to deploy a variety of voices of resistance that resound in the micropolitics of city life or transgress the institutionalized forms of non-contamination or non-contradiction characteristic of the politics of genre.[7]

In her *Song of Nyarloka* (1977), Oludhe Macgoye carries out a critique of the familiar categories that we use as guideposts for exploring the unfamiliar. Her suspicion of generic representations of the city, predicated upon book knowledge, is based on the differences between the African city she read about in her preparations for mission work in colonial Kenya and the realities of colonial zoning and curfews that constrained movement which she encountered on the ground upon her arrival. As *Song of Nyarloka* illustrates, such explicit attempts to map the African city only elide difference and succeed instead in revealing the writer's political and theoretical orientations. In contrast, a poetic venture into everyday rhythms and practices achieves important insights into the plural character of citiness and Africanness. It also resists developmentalist and statist representations of the African city that promote descriptions of culture and society as if they were fully observable phenomena, or attempts to make generalizations based on observation of "repetitive patterns of action in isolation from discourses that actors use in constituting and situating their action" (Tyler 1986, p. 123).

> For Nyarloka:
> The African city
> on which hundreds of thousands of words are expended
> in Harvard and Amsterdam,

---

6. Franco Moretti's reading of Jane Austen's novels and the Britain that they map invokes an appreciation of the manner in which a study of space in literature or literature in space provides for a literary geography that can be both centralizing or decentralizing (see Moretti 1998).
7. While Derrida considers the violence of institutionalized forms of non-contamination or non-contradiction characteristic of the 'law of genre', the same can be said for a politics of genre as it plays on the same claims to purity and partitioning of subjects and subject voices (see Derrida 1980).

> some tens of thousands
> at Limuru and Mindolo,
> never a one
> in Kariokor, Bahati or Manyatta,
> is very much like any other city.
>
> ...
> Writers will tell you
> you came to the city for the high life,
> because the lights and parks and windows are free,
> because you might win on the pools,
> see the races, dance at night-clubs,
> pick up expensive girls, change your style.
> One in ten of you, perhaps, has such a hope,
> one in twenty of you actually buys a dress
> at a sale in the bazaar,
> one in four hundred of you has ever been
> into the New Stanley Hotel for a cup of coffee,
> one in a thousand
> has once heard Sal Davis at a night-spot. (Oludhe Macgoye 1977, pp. 14-16)

Nyarloka's geo-poetics reveals the hidden Nairobi, the tough world that remains invisible to tourists and the colonial elite. She resists the naturalizing of urban space and gives a useful account of the colonial city by mapping the social inequalities and barriers that leave marks on the built environment, the human body and the body politic. These marks are evidence of the violence of generic forms that try to set rhythms that eliminate heterogeneity in the constitution of the African city. While Nyarloka remains attentive to the manipulative and proprietorial practices characteristic of city life, it is the tactical moves and the resilience of the city's inhabitants as they negotiate everyday life that she finds most interesting. Her poetics of everyday life marks its distance from traditional political and social formations by making audible or visible the desires, obsessions and fears of those who "don't mind a scratch or two, a tear or two, a rust-mark or two from the fence that does not bend" (Oludhe Macgoye 1977, p. 22).

Nyarloka's approach to the everyday is one that at once recognizes the many ways in which urban practices are disciplined and the clever tricks, insinuations and manoeuvres that are employed to escape the discipline. Her geo-poetic venture encourages modes of reading the city that map the transitivity/porosity characteristic of Nairobi, the multiple rhythms that mark the speeding up and slowing down of social life, the heterogeneity characteristic of urbanism, and the violent strategies and representations involved in containing such movements.

Urbicide: Building the Generic African City

> The act of representing others almost always involves violence to the subject of representation. (Said 1985,)

Moving on to post-colonial Nairobi, we encounter similar strategic exclusions that attempt to fix identity by regulating city rhythms and, in the process, create new contradictions that raise politically the problem of violence in post-colonial urban society. Today, Arjun Appadurai and James Holston, among others, will argue that:

> The city is a site for the formation and reformation of citizens but also serves as a war zone. A space in which processes of citizen formation find expression in collective violence. The city has always been a site of violent social and cultural confrontation. But in the contemporary world, the density of new social formations and superimposition of diverse cultural identifications produce a corresponding complexity of violence: urban terrorism ... gang shootings, death squads, vigilante lynching, private justice makings. (Appadurai & Holston 1996, p. 200)

While much can be said about Nairobi by paying attention to these "pre-given, irreducible or scripted" notions of violence (Bhabha 1994, p. 2) and their implications for city or national forms of citizenship, Nyarloka's explorations illustrate the political purchase of alternative conceptions of urban violence and the multiple in-between spaces and selves rendered visible or audible through a poetic rendering of the African city. Her mapping of African "elsewheres" and interstices (if I am to borrow the terminology employed by Achille Mbembe and Sarah Nuttall [2004]) demands that we pay attention to the systematic assault or killing of heterogeneity of urban life through practices that dictate everyday city rhythms and flows by determining the points of physical, social, economic and, therefore, political entry and exit; that is, the rhythmic urbicide characteristic of the city.

In resistance to the narrow conception of urbicide that confines it to the "killing or slaying of built environments" (Berman 1996) by exclusionary political programs[8], Nyarloka's geo-poetics in its textual exploration expands our conception of the killing of the urban to include the assault on the human body and its ability to move freely in both the "real" and the "poetic" city. This calls our attention to the politics of genre and the extent to which "the notion of genre purity in literary criticism serves much the same function as the notion of species purity in racist notions of humanity and history" (White 2003, p. 597). Such a treatment of the genre—city intertext is instructive as it helps us make conceptual distinctions between the "city" and the "urban", thus illustrating how certain textual representations and disciplinary practices in their constitution of the African city are actively involved in the killing of rhythms of plurality, or heterogeneity central to urban life.[9]

The implications for this kind of thinking are clear. It illustrates that certain modes of reading and writing about the African city or development planning, in their attempt to uphold a generic image of Africanness or citiness, do in actuality involve the killing of urban heterogeneity. If we follow Louis Wirth's (1996)[10]

---

8. For a more detailed engagement with the concept of urbicide, see Coward (2007).
9. Henri Lefebvre makes this city—urban distinction in the service of the same points in his book *The Urban Revolution* (2003, p. 43), where he notes that speaking of the urban involves looking beyond the city and encompasses a totality, an entire way of being, thinking and acting.
10. Wirth, in looking at urbanism as a distinctive mode of life, identifies three qualifying attributes of city populations; that is, their size, density and heterogeneity.

conception of urban life as heterogeneous existence, then any attempt to install the purity of genre, citiness or Africanness can be seen as the destruction of the conditions of possibility of urban life.

Applying such insights to Blixen's *Out of Africa* makes us aware of the many ways in which her writing and way of life are representative of colonial spatial formations that continue to determine Nairobi's built environment, racial distribution and the ability for social, economic and physical movement. If we consider the in-between space occupied by the garden and the culture of flowers, which was a marker of "high culture" among the British colonialists, then we can problematize the "naming of Nairobi" as the "Green City in the Sun", or Karen Blixen's desire to make a "name for herself" by introducing peonies into the colony. These naming practices are by no means innocent. They resonate well with the 1948 *Nairobi Master Plan for a Colonial Capital*, which provided ample scope for the application of Ebenezer Howard's "garden city" concept that conceives of urban planning as landscape gardening, thus preserving as much of the rural atmosphere as possible through restricting densities. This restriction of urban density was to be achieved through what the planners called a "humanistic bias" predicated upon economic determinants, implying that when enough Africans and Asians became as rich as the European population, Nairobi would be a fully integrated city. In the meantime, Europeans were to live in the low-density areas while the Africans lived in high-density areas (Thornton White *et al*. 1948). It is this kind of spatial formation that makes it possible for Blixen to talk of her African farm in which "the views were immensely wide and everything that you saw made for greatness, freedom, and *unequaled* nobility" (1984, p. 4). These low-density areas and green belts also create the conditions of possibility for the African high-density areas like Pumwani, which Nyarloka sees as the heart of Nairobi with:

> The long low houses ...
> the tarmac floors, parable of the city,
> suck in whatever is spilt upon them,
> beer, urine, sugar, ills and remedies. (Oludhe Macgoye 1977, p. 18)

The concept of a "green city" therefore legitimized the "whitening of privilege" through planning strategies and environmental or sanitation tropes that institutionalized the segregation of residential and commercial areas on the basis of class, caste (for Indians) and cultural habits.[11] The cultivation of this "colour bar" (both green and white) has had far-reaching effects on the interactions and life rhythms of Nairobi's European, Asian and African populations.

---

11. In her study of Nairobi townships in the context of race relations between 1912 and 1916, Anne Nangulu-Ayuku looks at how the colonial administration put in place a plan for the city where interaction between different races was limited. In this socially stratified and economically divided society, positions of power, wealth and influence coincided with divisions of race and colour such that Nairobi could be 'presented as a pyramid with Europeans at the apex, Asians in the middle and Africans at the base', and intergroup relations were based on mutual distrust and hostility (Nangulu-Ayuku 2000, p. 171).

What is at stake here is recognition that Nairobi is/was "poeticized by different subjects" (Mayol 1998, p. 13) along multiple lines of encounter and flight. With this in mind, it is possible to map the heterogeneous rhythms characteristic of Nairobi's urban culture in a manner attuned to the discourses that produce such rhythms. Such a rendering of the city follows from readings of the "urban reality" which resists the dichotomy between the real African city and one that is figural or imaginative, or the city and the country. Seeing Nairobi as a "collective assemblage"[12] — something produced by and productive of the memories, desires, signs and practices of those who inhabit it or the outsiders who partake of it — disrupts the image of a beautiful "Green City in the Sun" by highlighting the violence, disciplinary practices and exclusions necessary for the maintenance of this image. Basically, it involves asking: what is removed from the city? Which structures become illegal or which groups become socially aberrant?

A case in point is the Muoroto and Kibagare demolitions of informal settlements near the city centre in the early 1990s, where over 30,000 people were displaced. This official discourse that marks informal settlements as illegal can be traced back to the colonial era (Mitullah & Kibwana 1998, p. 191). For example, Kileleshwa was demolished in 1927 after European settlers in surrounding areas complained that it was a "breeding ground for crime and disease" (ibid.). Such unproblematic pathologizing of the informal settlements does not address the colonial rhythmic strategies of managing the African populations sanctioned by laws like the Vagrancy Act and Public Health Act, where Africans were allowed to enter the city only if they had a permit and stayed there as temporary sojourners without proper social amenities. It also fails to address the problematics of displacement occasioned by the expropriation practices of European settlers like Karen Blixen.

To achieve a critical perspective on the "Nairobian imaginary", it is important that we locate these urban subjectivities within a broader field of events that recognize the polyrhythmic character of "urbanism" as constitutive of the way of life in the city. This invites us to take note of the complexities of Nairobi's colonial past and the multiple global, local and rural connections that complicate urban temporality, and by extension spatiality. In order to do this successfully, we need to recognize the footprints of colonial cultural practices and how colonial rituals of mediation have correlates with the present. Here, Frantz Fanon's thought is important. It helps us come to terms with what he identified as the "presence of the colonizer within the colonized" (see Fanon 1967a, 1967b) and how this comes to bear on the post-colonial Nairobian imaginary.

African Rhythmanalysis: Poetic Cartography of an African Metropolis

Writing about otherness involves writing otherwise. (Mason 1990, p. 182)

---

12. By talking of cities as 'collective assemblages', I have in mind the interdependent roles, modes of creating and experiencing space, and subject positions that make the city emerge for us. This radically decentres the authorial practices and leads to an appreciation of the different genres and mediation practices at play in the city (see Deleuze & Guattari 1986, p. 22).

While there is no simple homology between the genre—city and the Africanness – citiness relationship in contemporary Africa, the above illustrations are a telling account of the inadequacy of the descriptive means at our disposal and the futility of attempts to capture the African condition in its totality. The African city, like the broader categories of Africa and the city, "escapes the grasp of both power and representation and allows itself to be evoked only through certain kinds of imagery" (Abbas 2003, p. 143).

For example, both colonial and post-colonial African cities have been built on discursive practices that either attempted to exclude or transform the African subject based on a particular version of modernity or the romanticization of nature. While these ambitious attempts at creating "the modern African" or "the authentic African" are to a large extent based on disciplinary practices that fix the rhythms of the city, there always exist multiple cultural and aesthetic tactics that pluralize urban space by complicating the rhythms of the city so as to include those "other figures of African modernity who exist both beneath the city and outside of its orders of visibility" (Mbembe & Nuttall 2004, p. 364).

With this in mind, there is a good reason for assuming that *rhythm* is a vital aspect of everyday life, with genre and the African city providing us with both a site and methodological basis for figuring the city on the basis of its rhythms. If we acknowledge that the body or the city's rhythms are always plural, cultural and social/political, then any reading of African cities/modernities should pay attention to present-day or historical "polyrhythmia" (the condition of plural rhythms) and the workings of genres through which we make sense of these rhythms.

These rhythms, as Ben Highmore illustrates, are the coordinates through which inhabitants and visitors frame and order the urban experience, and can either be "eurhythmic (ordered, harmonic and so on) or arrhythmic (discordant, irregular and so on)" (2005, p. 148). This incommensurability in modes of presence arising from the rhythmic, spatial and temporal (dis)junctures that populate urban space presents us with multiple African selves and others by unworking dominant spatial strategies and reading practices that articulate a rigid public—private split, or fixed friend—enemy relationships. As the above reading of Nyarloka *contra* Blixen illustrates, an attention to African urban polyrhythmia makes it possible for us to think differently about what it means to be African or a modern African, and what this means for people(s), modes of intelligibility, and those times and spaces that have remained at the margins of what is considered authentic African culture or thought. As Henri Lefebvre (1996, p. 88) reminds us in his writings about philosophy and the city, such an exploration is not aimed at producing a philosophy of the African city, but rather sees the city as a condition of possibility for African culture and philosophy or thinking.

The city therefore emerges as a space where the idea of Africanness is always being reinvented and contested, and with it the conception of authentic modes and rhythms of African life. If development planning and cultural governance in Karengata and Arusha aims at modernizing the Maasai by turning them into "proper urban" subjects, there are social and political groups that express a desire to return to traditional African values and practices. For example, the Mungiki — a Kikuyu-centric quasi-religious militia — denounces non-African (Kikuyu) cultural practices and has on numerous occasions been accused of the public stripping of women in trousers or miniskirts and running an underground economy that involves the manning of public washrooms, "tax collection" and extorting *matatu* (public transport) operators. The group has also had violent encounters with other vigilante groups like the Luo "Taliban" and their control over parts of the "Kosovo" area in Nairobi's Mathare slum contributes to forms of insecurity that reconfigure the city's slums and bus terminals as overwhelmingly masculine or ethnicized spaces.

What I find interesting about these two versions of Africanness (however removed from each other they may seem) is the moral cartography, rhythms, tensions and subjectivities that they enable. Under the rubric of Africanness, ethnic or modernist imaginaries are used to mark boundaries and legitimate violent practices in order to eradicate what is considered a cultural decadence (European miniskirts) or cultural retardation (Maasai nakedness).[13]

The violence occasioned by these arrhythmic conceptions of African city life suggests the need for a refiguring of categories of political viability in recognition of the African urban subject as "regularity in dispersion of positions of enunciation" (Foucault 1972, p. 27). It suggests a reworking of our ways of making sense of the world by being attentive to the disjunctive temporalities and co-presence characteristic of an everyday life in the city. Such a multiplicity of rhythms implies a rethinking of Africanness and the political along lines that do not only interrogate its essence but also its location.[14]

Read differently, the genres and practices that try to fix the character and location of the African self reveal the multiple registers within which the discourse of/on Africanness works as a spatializing practice that legitimates certain power arrangements and determine what becomes visible, audible or intelligible. Unless uncoded, these genres are condensed into acts of representation that silence certain voices as they attempt to discipline or control ambiguity by gradually raising the threshold of acceptability.

To exploit the conceptual and political richness of such revelations or events, it might be useful for us to evoke everyday life in the city[15] as a central trope for rethinking our conceptions of Africanness as this debunks the idea/image of

---

13. Mazrui (1975, p. 272) makes a similar reading of the Maasai situation under Operation Dress-Up and the irony of a Euro-Christian moral economy that aims at the liberation of Africans (Tanzanians) from practices that dehumanize the African body.
14. I find it instructive to invoke Michael Shapiro's engagement with Jean-Luc Nancy's conception of community as predicated on a politics that privileges multiple and disjunctive presences, as opposed to a community of unitary national culture arising from state scripting practices (see Shapiro 2000).
15. By privileging ephemeral, mass-produced artefacts — everyday objects whose very ubiquity and commonplace nature renders them almost invisible — looking at the city as one such artefact invites an appreciation of the banal aspects of urban life; the most repeated actions, most travelled journeys and inhabited spaces that make up day-to-day existence (see Highmore 2002, p. 2).

an Africa caught up in conditions of perpetual rurality (which in no way suggests a desirability or an attempt to "catch up" with Euro-American versions of modernity), and highlight the significance of urban cultural practices in the creation and the expression of a modern African identity (Nyairo 2005, p. 1). Everyday life is, then, a number of things; it is a refusal to privilege generic representations of African cities, and creates the conditions of possibility for multiple approaches to the African condition and the political by opening space for the consideration of plural genres, cultures and spaces as part of the African experience.

What such an enactment of politics suggests is the exploration of avenues of escape or lines of flight from closural politics, be it that of a nation-statist or colonial character emanating from a national elite, Eurocentric or Africanist moral point of view. Making such a refusal encourages us to read and write about Africa and the African city on a different plane. By acknowledging that the main problem in thinking about the post-colonial African city arises from the kind of questions used to interrogate categories of citiness and Africanness as they exist in their current forms, we are therefore summoned to raise new questions alongside those posed by urban theorists like Lewis Mumford (1937) and Louis Wirth (1938), who ask questions like "What is a city?" For the post-colonial, a more appropriate question would be "Which city?" or "Whose city?" as we attempt to defamiliarize ourselves with the definitions that limit our imaginations of the city. Similarly, the territorializing question "Where or what is Africa(n)?"[16], which locates Africanness in a certain part of the continent, in "perpetual rural cultures"[17] or in a past obliterated by colonialism, can be replaced by questions and rhetorical moves that aim at explicating everyday life as it is lived in different parts of Africa while remaining attentive to the heterogeneity of this lived space and, perhaps paradoxically, of lived time.

My main claim, therefore, is that such a rendering of Africa (and the city) creates the conditions of possibility for a literary, poetic and aesthetic errantry that enables us to explore a multitude of "micropolitical practices".[18] These moves, as I shall indicate more fully in the following section, enable an appreciation of alternative modes of attachment and contest modes of representing or transforming Africa or the city based on rigid rural/urban, African/European, traditional/modern, epistemology/aesthetics and real/imaginary dichotomies.

---

16. My main contention is that 'there is no African identity that could be designated by a single term or that could be named by a single word or subsumed under a single category. African identity does not exist as a substance. It is constituted, in varying forms, through a series of practices, notably *practices of the self*' (Mbembe 2002, p. 272). On the repartitioning of Africa in order to essentialize it, consider Hegel's treatment of Egypt that sees it as differentiated from 'Africa proper': sub-Saharan Africa, which is said to lack a history (Hegel 1991).

17. David Anderson and Richard Rathbone (2000) contest the idea of an Africa caught up in perpetual rurality.

18. Deleuze and Guattari (1987) oppose micropolitics to the politics of moralizing. Micropolitics is not defined by the smallness of its elements but by the nature of its mass. It is the form of political thought that responds to difference.

By focusing on this realm of activities designed to work on the affective registers of selves and groups, it becomes possible for us to experience the histories, anxieties and propulsions that are left out or considered second image in the dominant study of African cultures.

It is within such a formulation that it becomes possible for us to locate the "African problematic" (Korang 2004). That is, the places in the present where we can, and are enjoined to, interrogate what is actually different about and within Africa; where we can credit multiple Africas with imaginary and affective consistencies and inconsistencies in a manner that presupposes no ideological stability while contributing towards an experimentation with the possibility of becoming otherwise.[19]

Such a rendering of Africa facilitates an escape from fixed representations while opening space for a critical African cultural/political/philosophical project that considers those unacknowledged modes of "being" and "becoming" in contemporary Africa. Or, to put it otherwise, this shift from representation and recognition to invention is a political event which, according to Jacques Rancière, makes it possible for those people who have no proper place in the political community to nonetheless partake of the activities or imaginations of that community (Panagia 2000, p. 116). Such an aesthetic conception of politics is central to my attempt to interrogate practices that make voluble the voices that have been neglected in the academic construction of what qualifies as a politically viable voice in Africa.[20]

Rancière's approach to politics is compelling as it goes beyond raising new questions from the same old actors and opens up other spaces populated by other actors with their own set of questions. It also disposes us towards alternative ways of mapping the political where political thought and approaches to African culture and forms of expression are rendered as multi-genre as well as multi-ethnic fields of thinking. Similarly, the appreciation of the permeable boundary between epistemological and aesthetic modes of analysis that this approach enables has a profound impact on how we treat the politics of literary, visual and aural texts. For example, its employment of textual and visual forms that contain voices from diverse experiential spaces opposes a view of community premised on a fixed time—space relationship, and discourages any attempt at controlling ambiguity and the rigid categorization of entire cultural texts. At the same time, it also elucidates alternative understandings of the political through its appreciation of "unacknowledged worlds" by providing what Gilles Deleuze and Félix Guattari (1987) call "a line of flight" from dominant forms of collective expression.

---

19. Exploring a relational imaginary of Africa implies recognizing the existence of a totality (Africa) while at once renouncing any claims to sum it up or to possess it (see Glissant 1997, pp. 21, 32).
20. The extent to which a politics of aesthetics renders that which was previously invisible visible and the inaudible audible can be usefully mined in order to pluralize our readings of political contestation in/about Africa. The conceptual wealth of this mode of doing politics is developed in Shapiro (2006, p. ix).

Conclusion

In the guise of a conclusion, I would like to point to a particular type of poetics — rhythmanalysis — and how it highlights a polyphonic scenario where multiple voices speak the language of politics from various sites of enunciation.[21] According to Henri Lefebvre (2004, p. 23), "rhythmanalysis is a kind of poetics that performs a verbal action, which has an aesthetic import and concerns itself with temporalities and their relations within wholes".

In order to illustrate how such a poetics enables us to overcome conceptions of homogenous African temporality, it might be useful to make an exploration of the rhythms of Sheng[22], an urban sociolect that signifies a "linguistic third space" used to negotiate the multiple identities/differences that animate everyday life in Nairobi. Such an exploration, as opposed to statistical reading or ethnological studies, makes it possible for us to see how the African city is productive of a version of Africanness and politics that cannot be reduced to any single definitive category. It also illustrates how multiple fraternities are formed within urban space, and the sensibilities and violences developed to cope with this multilayered, multi-temporal way of life. A case in point is the ability of Nairobians to negotiate this urban space and multiple temporalities by being able to switch between English, Swahili (their "mother tongue") and Sheng or Engsh (a more anglicized form of Sheng), depending on who they are speaking to or where they are located (Bosire 2006, p. 192).

However, it is evident that Sheng-speaking and the various cultural practices that accompany it does not involve the emergence of an entirely "new" identity. Instead, it betrays the multiple sites through which the notion of Nairobianess has been mediated and poeticized and, at times, privileges one form of affiliation over all the others. It also illustrates the complex dynamics of encounter and the different ways in which different genres of expression and the cultural contexts of their reception and use take on meaning and change across political and cultural boundaries.

If looked at in terms of its rhythmicity, Sheng undoes common-sense geography of the city by creating new symbolic centres or through a repositioning of the city in various ways. For example, the multiple sites of Sheng production and consumption, like the *matatu* (public transport), *genge*, *ragga* and *kapuka* (local music), and *bazes* (hang-out joints), link easily with each other and other

---

21. On the polyvocality of the political, see Arditi (2003, p. 312).
22. While historical accounts of how Sheng came into being are beyond the purview of the present article, it is useful for us to consider some of the explanations put forth and relate them to our concern with Sheng as a spatial or rhythmic practice and its role in mediating estrangement in Nairobi. There are those who hold that Sheng emerged as a peer youth code in the low socio-economic Eastlands suburbs of Nairobi in the 1970s. According to Kembo-Sure (1992), the lack of privacy in these single- or two-roomed houses created the need for a code that enabled the youth to communicate among themselves while concealing their secrets from their parents. Other studies point out that a Sheng-like code existed as far back as the early 1930s in the Nairobi underworld among pickpockets (see Mazrui & Mphande 1990).

trends in popular culture. These provide complex integrative and interactive sites, or play on "shibboleths" and stasis as a way of keeping company among peers, marking territory and excluding outsiders. For example, the *baze* is to some extent based on exclusion and Sheng produced here is meant for peer communication/excommunication, while urban hip hop in Nairobi stands as a radically different Sheng project in terms of the mediation role it plays. Over the past few years, urban hip hop has been drawing an aural map of the city with different artistes narrating the neighbourhood or drawing a rave map of the city.

While Sheng developed as a tactical practice among the poor residents of Nairobi's Eastlands area, which served as the main site of Nyarloka's poetic investigations, today, it is widely spoken and remains a key determinant of one's entry into and participation in most official and "unofficial" spaces. As a transversal practice, Sheng-speaking makes it possible to code Nairobians on the basis of their competence and willingness to speak Sheng, or the ability to switch to other languages. For example, one can make an urban linguistic/cultural/economic map of the city by differentiating the Swahili-Sheng-speaking parts of the city (Mtaa, for example, in Pumwani) from the English-Engsh-speaking areas (Ubabini, for example, in Karen), which are associated with a westernized way of life or desire to be westernized (of the Babylon system). Thus, talking, producing or resisting Sheng can be read as a practice in the setting of urban rhythms through language-based self-fashioning.

What is evident from the above is that Sheng has moved from marginal spaces in the so-called "African locations" of the colonial city to nodal points and open spaces of everyday life in post-colonial Nairobi. It is part and parcel of the visual and aural cityscape, and is continuously reconfigured as it reconfigures Nairobi's rhythms and cultural imaginary. Thus, everyday life in the city is negotiated by the doubleness in ritual and rhythms characteristic of life in Nairobi. We have many Nairobians who speak Sheng, eat chapattis and masala (linking them to the Indian diaspora), wear second-hand designer clothes (from Europe and the USA) and are married once but wed twice, die once but have two funerals, one in the city and the other in the rural areas. This way of being in the world has its impact on the cultural landscape and built environment of Nairobi. Its signature is left on, sounds and rhythms of everyday life. The city as part of the African imaginary and the very existence of an African urban imaginary create the condition of possibility for rethinking the concepts, questions and practices through which we try to come to terms with the city, Africa or the city in Africa.

Acknowledgment

My thanks to Michael J. Shapiro for his careful reading of an early draft of this article and for organizing the "Genre and the City" seminar where most of the concepts explored were critically discussed.

References

Abbas, A. (2003) 'Cinema, the City, and the Cinematic', in Krause, L. & Petro, P. (eds), *Global Cities: Cinema, Architecture, and Urbanism in a Digital Age,* Rutgers University Press, New Brunswick, NJ, pp. 142-156.

Anderson, D. & Rathbone, R. (eds) (2000) *Africa's Urban Past,* James Currey, Oxford.

Appadurai, A. & Holston, J. (1996) 'Cities and Citizenship', *Public Culture,* vol. 8, pp. 187-204.

Appiah, K. A. (1993) *In My Father's House: Africa in the Philosophy of Culture,* Oxford University Press, New York.

Arditi, B. (2003) 'The Becoming-Other of Politics: A Post-Liberal Archipelago', *Contemporary Political Theory,* vol. 2, no. 3, pp. 307-325.

Bachelard, G. (1969) *The Poetics of Space,* trans. Jolas, M., Beacon Press, Boston.

Barthes, R. (1997) 'Semiology and the Urban', in Leach, N. (ed.), *Rethinking Architecture: A Reader in Cultural Theory,* Routledge, London, pp. 166-172.

Berman, M. (1996) 'Falling Towers: City Life After Urbicide', in Crow, D. (ed.), *Geography and Identity: Living and Exploring Geopolitics of Identity,* Maisonneuve Press, Washington, DC, pp. 172-192.

Bhabha, H. (1994) *Location of Cultures,* Routledge, London.

Blixen, K. (1984) *Out of Africa,* Penguin, Harmondsworth [first published 1937].

Bosire, M. (2006) 'Hybrid Languages: The Case of Sheng', in Arasanyin, O. F. & Pemberton, M. A. (eds), *Selected Proceedings of the 36th Annual Conference on African Linguistics,* Cascadilla Proceedings Project, Somerville, MA, pp. 185-193.

Bruno, G. (1997) 'Site-seeing: Architecture and the Moving Image', *Wide Angle,* vol. 19, no. 4, pp. 8-24.

Certeau, M. de (1984) *The Practice of Everyday Life,* trans. Rendall, S., University of California Press, Berkeley, CA.

Clifford, J. (1986) 'Introduction: Partial Truths', in Clifford, J. & Marcus, G. E. (eds), *Writing Culture: The Poetics and Politics of Ethnography,* University of California Press, Berkeley, CA.

Coward, M. (2007) '"Urbicide" Reconsidered', *Theory and Event,* vol. 10, no. 2.

Deleuze, G. & Guattari, F. (1986) *Kafka: Towards a Minor Literature,* trans. Polan, D., University of Minnesota Press, Minneapolis, MN.

Deleuze, G. & Guattari, F. (1987) *A Thousand Plateaus: Capitalism and Schizophrenia,* trans. Massumi, B., University of Minnesota Press, Minneapolis, MN.

Derrida, J. (1980) 'The Law of Genre', *Critical Inquiry,* vol. 7, no. 1, pp. 55-81.

Dinesen, I. [Karen Blixen] (1992) *Out of Africa,* Random House, New York [first published 1937].

Doty, R. (1996) 'The Double-Writing of Statecraft: Exploring State Responses to Illegal Immigration', *Alternatives,* vol. 21, no. 2, pp. 171-189.

Fabian, J. (1983) *Time and the Other: How Anthropology Makes Its Object,* Columbia University Press, New York.

Fanon, F. (1967a) *Black Skin, White Masks,* trans. Markmann, C. L., Grove Press, New York.

Fanon, F. (1967b) *The Wretched of the Earth,* trans. Farrington, C., Penguin, Harmondsworth.

Foucault, M. (1972) *The Archaeology of Knowledge and the Discourse on Language,* trans. Sheridan-Smith, A. M., Pantheon, New York.

Glissant, É. (1997) *Poetics of Relation,* trans. Wing, B., University of Michigan Press, Ann Arbor, MI.

Hake, A. (1977) *African Metropolis: Nairobi's Self-Help City,* Chatto and Windus for Sussex University Press, London.

Hegel, G. W. F. (1991) *The Philosophy of History*, trans. Sibree, J., Prometheus, Buffalo, NY.
Highmore, B. (2002) *Everyday Life and Cultural Theory: An Introduction*, Routledge, London.
Highmore, B. (2005) *Cityscapes: Cultural Readings in the Material and Symbolic City*, Palgrave Macmillan, New York.
Howard, E. (1898) *To-morrow: A Peaceful Path to Real Reform*, Routledge, London.
Howard, E. (1902) *Garden Cities of To-morrow*, 2nd edn, Faber and Faber, London.
Kembo-Sure (1992) 'The Coming of Sheng', *English Today*, vol. 32, pp. 26-28.
Korang, K. L. (2004) 'Where Is Africa? When Is the West's Other? Literary Postcoloniality in a Comparative Anthropology', *Diacritics*, vol. 34, no. 2, pp. 38-61.
Kurtz, J. R. (1998) *Urban Obsessions, Urban Fears: The Postcolonial Kenyan Novel*, Africa World Press, Lawrenceville, NJ.
Lavine, S. D. & Karp, I. (1991) 'Introduction: Museums and Multiculturalism', in Karp, I. & Lavine, S. D. (eds), *Exhibiting Cultures: The Poetics and Politics of Museum Display*, Smithsonian Institution Press, Washington, DC.
Lefebvre, H. (1996) *Writings on Cities*, trans. and ed. Kofman, E. & Lebas, E., Basil Blackwell, Oxford.
Lefebvre, H. (2003) *The Urban Revolution*, trans. Bononno, R., University of Minnesota Press, Minneapolis, MN.
Lefebvre, H. (2004) *Rhythmanalysis: Space, Time and Everyday Life*, trans. Elden, S. & Moore, G., Continuum, London.
Mason, P. (1990) *Deconstructing America: Representation of the Other*, Routledge, London.
Mayol, P. (1998) 'Living', in de Certeau, M., Giard, L. & Mayol, P., *The Practice of Everyday Life. Volume 2: Living and Cooking*, trans. Tomasik, T. J., University of Minnesota Press, Minneapolis, MN.
Mazrui, A. A. (1970) 'The Robes of Rebellion: Sex, Dress, and Politics in Africa', *Encounter*, vol. 34, no. 2, pp. 19-30.
Mazrui, A. A. (1975) *Soldiers and Kinsmen in Uganda: The Making of a Military Ethnocracy*, Sage, Beverly Hills, CA.
Mazrui, A. M. & Mphande, L. (1990) 'How Is a Codemixer's Grammar Organized? Evidence from Sheng', *21st Annual Conference on African Linguistics*, 12-14 April, University of Georgia, Athens, GA.
Mbembe, A. (2002) 'African Modes of Self-Writing', *Public Culture*, vol. 14, no. 1, pp. 239-273.
Mbembe, A. & Nuttall, S. (2004) 'Writing the World from an African Metropolis', *Public Culture*, vol. 16, no. 3, pp. 347-372.
Ministry of Lands and Housing, Physical Planning Department & City Council of Nairobi, City Planning Department (2005) *Karengata Local Physical Development Plan 2005-2015*, http://www.klda.or.ke/docs/LPDP%20Report%20final%20version%20III%20Roman%20pages.doc.
Mitchell, W. J. T. (1995) 'Translator Translated — Interview with Cultural Theorist Homi Bhabha', *Artforum*, vol. 33, no. 7, pp. 80-84.
Mitullah, W. & Kibwana, K. (1998) 'A Tale of Two Cities: Policy, Law and Illegal Settlements in Kenya', in Fernandes, E. & Varley, A. (eds), *Illegal Cities: Law and Urban Change in Developing Countries*, Zed Books, London, pp. 191-212.
Moretti, F. (1998) *Atlas of the European Novel, 1800-1900*, Verso, New York.
Mudimbe, V. Y. (1988) *The Invention of Africa: Gnosis, Philosophy, and the Order of Knowledge*, Indiana University Press, Bloomington, IN.
Mumford, L. (1937) 'What Is a City?' *Architectural Record*, vol. 82, pp. 59-62.
Nangulu-Ayuku, A. (2000) 'Politics, Urban Planning and Population Settlement: Nairobi, 1912-1916', *Journal of Third World Studies*, vol. 17, no. 2, pp. 171-204.

Nyairo, J. (2005) '"Modify": *Jua Kali* as a Metaphor for Africa's Urban Ethnicities and Cultures', *Mary Kingsley Zochonis Lecture*, School of Oriental and African Studies, University of London, 2 July.

Oludhe Macgoye, M. (1977) *Song of Nyarloka and Other Poems*, Oxford University Press, Nairobi.

Panagia, D. (2000) 'Dissenting Words: A Conversation with Jacques Rancière', *Diacritics*, vol. 30, no. 2, pp. 113-126.

Reynolds, B. (2003) *Performing Transversally: Reimagining Shakespeare and the Critical Future*, Palgrave Macmillan, New York.

Said, E. (1978) *Orientalism*, Vintage Books, New York.

Said, E. (1985) 'In the Shadow of the West', *Wedge*, vol. 7-8, pp. 4-11.

Schneider, L. (2006) 'The Maasai's New Clothes: A Developmentalist Modernity and Its Exclusions', *Africa Today*, vol. 53, no. 1, pp. 101-129.

Shapiro, M. J. (1985) 'Toward a Politicized Subject: Peter Handke and Language', *Boundary 2*, vol. 13, no. 2/3, pp. 393-418.

Shapiro, M. J. (2000) 'National Times and Other Times: Re-thinking Citizenship', *Cultural Studies*, vol. 14, no. 1, pp. 79-98.

Shapiro, M. J. (2006) *Deforming American Political Thought: Ethnicity, Facticity and Genre*, University Press of Kentucky, Lexington, KY.

Thiong'o, N. wa (1981) *Writers in Politics*, Heinemann, London.

Thornton White, L. W., Silberman, L. & Anderson, P. R. (1948) *Nairobi: Master Plan for a Colonial Capital*, Her Majesty's Stationery Office, London.

Tyler, S. (1986) 'Post-modern Ethnography: From Document of the Occult to Occult Document', in Clifford, J. & Marcus, G. (eds), *Writing Culture: Poetics and Politics of Ethnography*, University of California Press, Berkeley, CA.

White, H. (2003) 'Anomalies of Genre: The Utility of Theory and History for the Study of Literary Genres', *New Literary History*, vol. 34, pp. 597-615.

Wirth, L. (1938) 'Urbanism as a Way of Life', *American Journal of Sociology*, vol. 44, no. 1, pp. 1-24.

Wirth, L. (1996) 'Urbanism as a Way of Life', in Le Gates, R. T. & Stout, F. (eds), *The City Reader*, Routledge, New York.

Wirth-Nesher, H. (1996) *City-Codes: Reading the Modern Urban Novel*, Cambridge University Press, Cambridge.

Centrifugal Bostons and Competing Imaginaries in *Mystic River*

Nicolette Rowe

Dennis Lehane's novel *Mystic River* and Clint Eastwood's film of the same name navigate between various binaries to produce politically assiduous critiques of urban life that defy genre and film noir in particular. Both Bakhtin's concept of heteroglossia and Lefebvre's notion of abstract space resonate with the film's cinematic techniques and *mise en scène* in ways that enable the viewer to draw meaning from the film that cannot be attributed to the plot itself. The film decenters urban experiences and blurs traditional boundaries towards a tragic effect, and perhaps intentionally fails to fully represent the pain and confusion that its characters embody. The cinematic refusal to arrive at any definitive ethical conclusions contributes to the biting critique of anti-ideal urban life as it is portrayed within a particular Boston neighborhood.

Introduction

Now why should the cinema follow the forms of theater and painting rather than the methodology of language, which allows wholly new concepts of ideas to arise from the combination of two concrete denotations of two concrete objects? (Eisenstein, quoted on *They Shoot Pictures Don't They?*)

In both the novel and the film version of *Mystic River*, the plot covers the story of three childhood friends — Jimmy Markum (Sean Penn), Sean Devine (Kevin Bacon), and Dave Boyle (Tim Robbins) — who are reluctantly "reunited" as adults when Jimmy's 19-year-old daughter Katie is murdered. While some aspects of what turns out to be a murder story are central to the plot in Clint Eastwood's film *Mystic River* (2003), as the plot develops, the film's mood and tonalities evoke the film noir genre. However, the film modifies, if not deforms, many classic characteristics of film noir, because while the typical noir film focuses on the absence of communitarian sentiments, *Mystic River* dwells on, while complicating, notions of "community", in this case a fictional Boston community, "the Flats". While the tension between "real" versus "imagined" communities in the film is best analyzed using Ben Highmore's realist methodology, which acknowledges the convergence of the textual and the actual (Highmore 2005, p. 154), we can arrive at a more politically assiduous understanding of how this film depicts urban space when we analyze it alongside Dennis Lehane's (2001) novel of the same name. Lehane's novel exceeds Highmore's realist approach by connecting spatio-temporal resonances (well treated by Highmore) of the historically situated dynamics of Boston communities with the specific experiences of the characters whose interactions effect the plot.

Given that the film relies heavily on various collective and individual accounts of the past in order to portray the present, it is appropriate to use the genre of the novel in order to fill in gaps, as it were, if we are to agree with M. M. Bakhtin's (1981, p. 29) assertion that "only in the novel have we the possibility of an authentically objective portrayal of the past as the past". In addition, Bakhtin's concept of heteroglossia, or the existence of multiple contending voices, complicates and emphasizes tensions in the city—countryside dichotomy, which, contrary to Highmore's reading, do not result in a collapse of meaning for them both (Highmore 2005, p. 127). While the novel exposes tensions inherent in the spatial and temporal aspects of urban space, this analysis will attend to the mechanisms by which the film version decenters the viewers' perceptions of the "urban". Paying particular attention to the projection of cosmopolitan interests onto the landscapes of Boston neighborhoods, the film lends itself to a critical reading of abstract spaces, or spaces that are homogenous, administratively policed, and hierarchically organized. In particular, I emphasize the way Sean's character is complicit with the bureaucratic agenda of abstract space. Wholly apart from his personality characteristics, his occupation as a State Homicide detective necessarily suggests that he is an occupier or "carrier" of abstract space.

Parallel Realities and Contending Voices

Recalling James Sanders' argument in his *Celluloid Skyline: New York and the Movies* (2003) that there are two New Yorks, one real and one dreamed, each with its own history, it is useful to analyze the two Bostons portrayed in *Mystic River*. Sanders describes this urban dream of New York as a parallel universe of sorts, much like the parallel universes described by two of the characters in *Mystic River*, Dave Boyle and Sean Devine. Dave Boyle sees his own history as consisting of parallel lives led by "the boy who escaped from the wolves" (the wolves being the child molesters who abducted him at a young age)[1] and the real Dave Boyle whom the community acknowledges. The other instance of a parallel universe occurs at the end of the film when Sean suggests that "none of this is real", and that — hypothetically — both he and Jimmy had got in the fateful sedan so many years ago and are in actuality stuck in a cellar below the earth.

---

1. Unless otherwise stated, all *Mystic River* quotes are taken from the film version.

Both the film and the novel allude to multiple realities, which become understandable if we invoke Bakhtin's concept of heteroglossia and note that Jimmy, Dave, and Sean possess distinct voices and urban desires, which constitute the complexity and contradictions inherent in Boston's urban spaces. This heteroglossic representation of Boston is related to the constant movement between metaphor and reality in both the film and the novel, which makes apparent a dynamic relationship between urban imaginaries and urban realities. Each character works in one way or another towards the creation of their ideal city, and their daily discursive practices reflect their urban desires. Jimmy's urban utopia is one in which he has the ability to protect his family and maintain control over circumstances that affect their well-being. However, while Jimmy's power afforded by his family and business connections (a euphemism for networks in the Irish mob) allows him to maneuver within various abstract spaces typically limited to state actors such as the Massachusetts state police, his parallel criminal investigation of his daughter's murder runs counter to his urban imaginary. Jimmy's attempts to rectify urban wrongs are used as self-justification for murdering both "Just Ray" Harris and Dave Boyle. Indeed, throughout the film, private interests are displaced onto public objects and rationalized in terms of public interests (Lasswell 1977, p. 75). The murders are interpreted as payment for the time "stolen" from him — in Jimmy's mind, both "Just Ray" and Dave robbed him of time with his now deceased wife and murdered daughter. The result of Jimmy acting according to his urban desires is the creation of an urban reality that undermines the very values he sought to protect. Jimmy's murder of "Just Ray" and Dave results in the further disruption of families. Ray and Brendan Harris are deprived of their father and the truth behind his disappearance, and Dave's wife and son are deprived of their husband and father respectively. In contrast, Dave's urban utopia is one in which he can undo his past and recover his true self, a person he claims disappeared the day he agreed to get in the car with two child molesters. As an adult some 30 years later, Dave kills a child molester in hopes of masking unpalatable thoughts in his past, an action he deems as killing the vampire within him. Even after Dave murders a "real" child molester, he is unable to exorcise the internal or "imaginary" child molester within his conscious. Sean's voice or contribution to this heteroglossic account is unique, and is discussed in detail below.

Contested Community and Urban Anxieties

The community or neighborhood is the key geographic unit of urban analysis for both Lehane and Eastwood. It serves as the major site of contention throughout the novel and the film. While Jimmy clings to a romanticized definition of a perfect Irish Catholic family, Dave nostalgically hopes to recover an affordable community that has since been threatened by centrifugal forces such as globalizing capital. Dave's urban reality is a community in which blue-collar workers are becoming increasingly threatened by rising real estate prices. He conspicuously and hypothetically suggests that if a crime wave were to sweep across the area, the yuppies may no longer find moving into the city so desirable. Dave's urban anxieties stem from a sense of inevitable and impending urban homogenization and a linear progression of cookie-cutter houses as a symptom of global pressures to sell out individuality *en masse*. These anxieties stem from modernity's active unevenness in terms of both architecture and the use of space. Dave and his friends speak about the conversion of housing complexes and apartments into malls and commercial units in a way that laments the onset of what Sartre deems the "individual impersonality of the universal" (Dimendberg 2004, p. 32). Dave expresses his angst towards the perceived aggressions of the community outsiders in his inner dialogue: "They snapped up the brick three-deckers that suddenly weren't three-deckers anymore but Queen Annes" (Lehane 2001, p. 42).

If Jimmy and Dave embody two distinct and conflicting imaginaries and realities of urban space and agency, Sean provides the third "voice" to the urban and heteroglossic film/novel bricolage. While Jimmy and Dave's urban desires and anxieties are intimately related to their own personal tragedies, Sean, in contrast, is both a bridge character and a carrier of abstract space; the vocation of State Homicide detective conveys universal valuing postures, which Sean assumes when he literally stands and acts in the spaces of bureaucratic politics. Because Sean is perpetually "at work" in the film, his home, public spaces, and his office are collapsed into homogenous abstract space or "workspace". Thus, his desires and spatial practices reflect and influence the state's practice of law enforcement in the city of Boston. Sean worries less about "neighborhood" issues such as yuppy infiltration and "family" issues such as having a close relationship with his wife than he does about more abstract concerns such as the crime rate.[2]

Though not explicitly stated, Jimmy's family connections and early involvement with organized crime and Dave's victimization as a child precludes the opportunity for their entry into the state police force, and subsequently limits their ability to participate in the abstract spaces that affect their personal lives. Sean grew up in the slightly more affluent area known as "the Point". The security afforded by his family's financial well-being enabled him to turn his attention to the state police department and focus on abstract principles such as keeping the streets safe and ensuring as much retributive justice as possible. As a bridge character, whose identity is suspended between the local scene and the abstract space generated by his vocation, Sean uses a degree of flexibility in applying the norms of his vocation in order to mediate among the state police, Jimmy, and Dave. While Sean does his best to disqualify Dave from the list of suspects in Katie Markum's murder investigation, his ability to "protect" Dave is limited because of his need to maintain an air of objectivity around Sergeant Whitey Powers and the "staties". On the other hand, finding Katie's murderer was the only thing that Sean could have done to prevent Jimmy from murdering Dave, and for this

---

2. For most of the duration of the film, Lauren, Sean's wife, is referred to as 'missing' — she has taken their son to some undisclosed location. Although she returns and reunites with Sean at the close of the film, it is implied that their marriage has suffered due to some combination of neglect, apathy, and preoccupation with work on Sean's behalf.

purpose it seems that Sean has cracked the case just hours too late. Sean's reaction on discovering that Jimmy murdered Dave is somewhat ambiguous. While he vows to "get" Jimmy, as it were, there is no concrete indication that Sean is genuinely and rigorously pursuing the case.

The South Boston neighborhood portrayed in the film and novel represents that which is degenerate and inescapable, yet it continues to be a source of pride and accomplishment for those who live there. And because Eastwood's *mise en scène* provides insights that escape the perceptions of the characters, the film shows the viewers forces at work that operate outside of the motivations of the individual characters. For example, the Boston police are ridiculed by the staties and are half-jokingly accused of botching evidence relevant to Katie's murder case. However, the fact that the fears of infiltration, homogenization, and gentrification have existed for generations suggests that there is still a Boston, or sections of Boston, that citizens deem worth claiming, identifying with, and protecting. Boston Red Sox games repeatedly provide occasions for members of the community to gather together at bars and in houses in Boston. Multiple layers of pride and self-identification are demonstrated by various logos worn by individuals and displayed on stores and buildings. Jimmy Markum's store has a Budweiser sign, an American flag, and a Red Sox symbol. This identification of self with a confusing mixture of love, hate, and indifference to the state, city of Boston, and neighborhoods in South Boston results in a deployment of various and contested meanings of "community" and criteria for belonging to such a community in both the novel and film.

Centrifugal Urban Space and Distinct Communities

The overall representation of small communities in Boston, including the Flats and the Point, fits the bill of microenvironments competing against one another, each a distinguishable community. The cinematography features a few aerial shots that clearly identify the setting as Boston; however, the shots are not extremely menacing, towering, or panoptic in nature. The camera often moves forward in a relatively low and horizontal manner, zooming in on the neighborhoods featured in the film. This is in sharp contrast to photo-documentary-like cliché shots pronouncing the hierarchy of the city and aimed at focusing the viewer on the center of the city, and immediately associating the film and the plot with a universalistic notion of Boston (Mumford 1961, p. 495). Instead, the tranquility of the Mystic River is surveyed in some aerial shots; a tranquility that turns out to be cosmetic, yet which undoubtedly anchors the community or neighborhood as the main unit of representation in the film and the novel. This does not mean that the city as a whole is not represented or that the suburbs are omitted from these accounts; it simply means that Boston is represented in such a way that emphasizes centrifugal forces. The suburbs, for instance, are not directly represented, but are referred to. As a result, ideas about them are integral to the city's identity anywhere along the spectrum from real to imagined:

"What the suburb retains today is largely its original weaknesses: snobbery, segregation, status seeking, political irresponsibility" (Mumford 1961, p. 502). The pride in one's neighborhood within Boston accompanied by the critiquing of undesirable outside characteristics, evident in dialogues, helps define collective notions of neighborhoods, suburbs, and the city center. This tension between inside and outside as well as centripetal and centrifugal is orchestrated by the film's use of the two kinds of cinematic space discussed by Noel Burch in *Theory of Film Practice* (1995). The characters and the neighborhood landscapes are often directly represented on the screen, and are thus examples of what Burch considers on-screen cinematic space, which includes "everything that can be perceived on the screen by the eye" (Burch 1995, p. 17). On the other hand, suburbs, the city center, and global forces that are not directly represented fall into what Burch calls off-screen space. In sum, the film is a decentered mode of representation in that it directly represents the outskirts of Boston while implicating the center urban spaces using off-screen cinematic space.

The main unit of identification and pride in *Mystic River* is not the city of Boston or the state, but the neighborhood. The blue-collar area known as the Flats is contrasted to the more affluent Point. The informal nature of parties, celebrations, and mourning in the Flats is quite different from the planned get-togethers in the Point: "In the Point they had block parties, sure, but they were always planned, the necessary permits obtained" (Lehane 2001, p. 22). The sense of community is accompanied by the fear of change. Dave laments to himself that there are just so few of those people left from the old days. The "loss" of community is to be feared from all sides — drugs, the police forces, jail, the suburbs, and other states. From Dave's point of view, the neighborhood is where all of the people who *belong* together live (Lehane 2001, p. 394). A distinct approach to the "protection" of the neighborhood comes from the logic of organized crime. Gratitude to the "governing presence" (Lehane 2001, p. 392) in the Flats comes in the form of "an envelope here, a cake, a car there" (p.393), seen by many as a reward for "keeping them safe" (ibid.) Jimmy's possessive and protective behavior over his family is a microcosm of the sense of entitlement and ownership of the Irish organized networks within the neighborhood. The parallel investigation of Katie's murder by the Savage brothers is received exceptionally well by the community. When Katie's two friends are questioned by detectives Sean Devine and Whitey Powers of State Homicide, they begrudgingly confess the name of Katie's boyfriend after mumbling that they have already told the Savages, implying that the girls trust the Savage brothers more than they do the state police. They also correctly assume that the police will be wrong and hasty in implicating Brendan Harris in the murder.

Continuation of Past into Present

It is through memory that the past exists in the present. That past has a more persistent purchase on the present for those who remain within the same place throughout their lives.[3] Because Dave, Jimmy, and Sean grew up together and continue to live in Boston, the existence of their pasts in their presents is especially vivid. The small neighborhoods that each character grew up in allowed for reputations and legacies to develop and stay with the individual. Dave has the reputation of being "damaged goods", a view which becomes general information that investigators think relevant during the investigation of Katie Markum's murder. Dave's other reputation is being a high-school baseball star, a legacy that lives on through his marriage and family life. Dave Boyle is unable to externally and internally come to terms with his own tragic past. In the opening scene of the film, young Dave, Jimmy, and Sean are playing hockey in their street and begin writing their names on a slab of wet cement. Two men claiming to be police officers reprimand the boys and demand that Dave get in the car. In the following scene, the camera focuses on Dave's pleading face peering out the back of the sedan, and the camera remains still as the sedan moves farther down the road and out of sight. As an adult, the cityscape reminds Dave of the trauma that haunts his adult life — his experience of molestation as a child. Dave is shown walking with his son as he comes across the street where he played hockey as a child, and gives pause while glancing at his name, half inscribed into the cement. The state police also keep a "memory" of Dave's past, using Dave's victim status as grounds for making him a suspect in Katie's murder case. The knowledge that Dave was a victim as a child garners suspicion rather than sympathy — as Whitey Powers of State Homicide reasons, "on paper Dave is as good as in jail".

Jimmy's previous reputation as the slick 19-year-old criminal who commanded operations like clockwork continues to follow him long after he has abandoned those activities. Even the issue of Jimmy's criminality makes it into the questions thought relevant in the criminal investigation of his daughter. In the end, however, Jimmy also fails to "escape" his past, returning instead to the same illegal mob activities he polished at the age of 19. Although Sean is the exception in having been able to "escape" the old neighborhood in which he grew up, as he assumes the lead investigator position in Katie Markum's murder, he realizes that his memory of his past and the old friendships, which he has subsequently attempted to deny, continue to affect him. As a State Homicide detective, Sean represents a deformation of the typical American hard-boiled crime fiction variety. He fails to appear as tough, cool, and lecherous, as is the case with such hard-boiled private detectives as Dashiell Hammett's Sam Spade, and he is not as morally grounded and contemplative as Raymond Chandler's Philip Marlow. In novels, comics, and films, typical hard-boiled types, including Spade and Marlow, are depicted as "users of space" (McCann 1999, p. 172) whose daily spatial practices demand that they creatively navigate through heterogeneous and often dangerous urban space. Sean deforms typical film noir spatial tropes by limiting his use of space to abstract space. For the most part,

---

3. Just as the pasts of the main characters 'haunt' their present realities, Bergson (1990, p. 150) suggests that '[p]ractically we perceive only the past, the pure present being the invisible progress of the past gnawing into the future'.

his use of space is mechanical; his pursuit of criminals is comparatively passive, static, and passionless.

The existence of the past in the present is also conveyed by Eastwood's cinematic tropes. Several shots feature cars driving away, which are captured from the back — for example, shots showing Dave (first as a boy and later as an adult) looking out of the rear window towards the camera. His facial expressions are a call for help, and the camera is static while the car drives farther away into the distance. While in the first instance Dave is held captive by two law enforcement imposters, as an adult he is taken into custody by the state police. Hockey sticks are featured at the beginning of the film to symbolize the childhood innocence of Jimmy, Dave, and Sean, while the hockey sticks featured at the end of the film are symbolic of childhood perversion; it is implied that Ray Harris and Johnny O'Shea used hockey sticks to kill Katie Markum.

Imagined Borders in the Negotiation of City Space

People and organizations such as the state and Boston city police departments act on and respond according to both concrete evidence and metaphors, stereotypes, and assumptions based on invisible yet not quite arbitrary divisions within the city. Katie's murder constitutes a failure of the justice system, and it is at this point that the "frogmen" are called forth to penetrate the Mystic River, and helicopters are deployed to aerially map and search the park. The underbelly of the city is a prevalent theme; examples include the sewer that swallowed all of the neighborhood's balls, the cellar in the woods where Dave was kept for four days, and the basement where Katie's body was kept. Each of these examples symbolizes figurative or actual death.

Borders, intersections, and roads are depicted as dangerous and contentious in both the book and film. The general recognition of borders as such has to do with lawful jurisdiction as well as the collective understanding of boundaries by the residents. For example, the reason that Jimmy Markum's girl Katie and her two friends decide to go to the Last Drop, a bar located in the Flats, probably has to do with the fact that they are 19-year-olds and would not be admitted by many of the upper-crust and thus more strict establishments. Three "East Bucky" girls found dancing on the bar counters in the Flats are described as an uncommon occurrence; and their sex, age, and behavior does make them appear quite out of place in the bar scene portrayed in the film. Jimmy's store is also located at a crucial border — the East Bucky Flats/Point line of demarcation. According to Lehane, the novel's author—narrator, the reason the store has never been robbed, and perhaps one of the reasons Jimmy has been able to maintain his law-abiding behavior after getting out of jail, has to do with the plain fact that no one was so dumb as to try to rob a store on the East Bucky Flats/Point line (Lehane 2001, p. 72). Perhaps Jimmy would not have had the luxury of "staying straight" if he did not have the family and friend support and the backing of many who were far from straight, including the Savage brothers who were just "plain scary" (Lehane 2001, p. 79). The location of Katie Markum's murder is also on the line between state and city jurisdiction, which ultimately results in Sean from State Homicide handling the investigation. Her car was found on Sydney Street, which is city jurisdiction, but the blood trail led to Penitentiary Park, which is state jurisdiction (Lehane 2001, p. 81).

While the film articulates some aspects of Boston's racial/spatial order, the movements of the characters, perceptions of class, personality, and the nature of social interactions are further implicated in the novel. Most importantly, the genre of the novel allows a racial history of Boston to be told and connected with the storyline in ways that the film only begins to accomplish. For example, in the novel, a short description of how the "desegregation busing" of the 1970s affected Boston's urban landscape informs our understanding of the tensions between those who "belong" to the neighborhood and those outside of it. Jimmy and Val are two characters that grew up in a relatively poor area, the Flats, and were troublemakers in their school. Their punishment of sorts was to get bused halfway across the city to a mostly black school, Carver (Lehane 2001, p. 30). This educational path is much different than that experienced by Sean, who lived in the richer Point. He was recruited to attend a Latin school where "opportunity" awaited him. Marita, Jimmy's first wife, is described as a Puerto Rican beauty, and their union was thought strange and unconventional even for those who were considered rough around the edges. Jimmy's marriage was commonly perceived as strange and *exotic* — he was the man who "married a Puerto Rican chick, and one from the outside neighborhood, too" (Lehane 2001, p. 93). Racial alliances also play a part in the divisions among gangs and neighborhood borders — the drug dealers forged deals with the Vietnamese gangs in Rome Basin "to keep the gooks out" (Lehane 2001, p. 392). Boston has a long history of immigration and ethnic feuding, but according to the narrator, there is logic to the bloodbath. After the prison closed and the cattle boom ended, the Irish immigrant wave followed the Italian one in twice the numbers (Lehane 2001, p. 398).

Jimmy and his family, like many others in the Flats, are Irish Catholic. This becomes apparent through the symbolic and real events surrounding life and death, and monumental events along the way such as Nadine's first Communion. According to Jimmy, the first Communion is an event in a Catholic child's life that should not be missed and that must be done properly (Lehane 2001, p. 87). While Sean is also Catholic, his participation in these Catholic milestones is less frequent and more out of obligation than pride and tradition. He admits to only seeing much of his family, including his parents, at weddings and wakes (Lehane 2001, p. 200). The Celtic cross is an Irish symbol that appears several times in the film, first as a tattoo on Jimmy's back, and second as a suggestion for Katie's tombstone: "Maybe a Celtic cross", the tombstone salesman says, "a choice that is quite popular with ... an awful lot of people these days" (Lehane 2001, p. 31). Being Irish and Catholic in Boston is as much a basis for marking life's milestones for individuals and families as it is a basis for making snap judgments about class or area of residence. While Irish Catholic is an "inside" characteristic of South Boston neighborhoods, its role in the larger picture of Boston is one of assumed lower socio-economic status and racial inferiority. However, the social and cultural stigma of being Irish pales in comparison to that of being African American. One of the investigators, Martin Freil, admits his sympathy bias: "You know what I like even less than ten-year-old black boys getting shot by bullshit gang-war crossfire ... Nineteen-year-old white girls getting murdered in my park" (Lehane 2001, p. 145).

References to desiring the consumption of loved ones are an example of what Barthes would call eroticism — a type of sociality that includes an encounter with the other, becoming the other, and obsessive compulsions (Krause & Petro 2003, p. 145). Jimmy's particular commitment to his daughter conjures Freudian analogies; one explanation being that in many ways Katie was his favorite, more intensely loved than any female in his life, including both wives, because of the father—daughter bond and their experience of loss and loneliness during the time they spent alone after Marita, Katie's mother, died. His duties did not end after her death because he felt that it was his responsibility to make sure that she be remembered as she was, extremely neat. Katie's death does not paralyze Jimmy, but instead motivates him to search for her killer while making sure all of the details of Katie's funeral are in order (Lehane 2001, p. 218). In addition to an implied eroticism between the father and the daughter and hints of jealousy on behalf of Annabeth, Katie's mother-in-law, there is also a strong association between strength, loyalty, and (a metaphorical) cannibalism between Annabeth and Jimmy. They love each other so much they want to eat each other (Lehane 2001, p. 385). They regard this familial cohesion as strength, whereas everyone else surrounding them is weak. Dave's insistence on comparing himself to a vampire suggests that his simultaneous desire to "infect" someone else is accompanied by the desire to exorcize whatever it was that got inside of him when he was molested as a boy. Bakhtin (1981, p. 101) defines eroticism as presupposing "a deliberate opposition of what is alien to what is one's own, the otherness of what is foreign is emphasized, savored, as it were, and elaborately depicted against an implied background of one's own ordinary and familiar world". Eroticism is thus as relevant to concrete urban fears such as economic and social encroachment on the community from centripetal (moving from the suburbs) and centrifugal (moving from the city center) forces, and the spread of homogeneous abstract space as it is to romantic encounters.

While there are certain aspects of the film that are reminiscent of Jules Dassin's *The Naked City* (1948), which features a disaster narrative, aerial views, street scenes, and humanizing narration that equate violence to "the rule of the land" and a cohesive agent, *Mystic River* limits the role of violence as a cohesive agent (Mumford 1961, p. 67). While the Catholic traditions of funerals and wakes and the "reuniting" of Jimmy, Dave, and Sean as a result of Katie's murder could be interpreted as a violence that produces cohesive effects, the long-term consequences of the acts of violence in the film are disruptive, and result in the disintegration of families and the dissolution of trust. The novel's perpetual return to the South Boston neighborhood and the past lives of its main characters exposes the layers of history rooted in crime as witnessed by the historiography of Boston envisioned as radiating both spatially and temporally outwards from Penitentiary Park. The tension between the dichotomies of hope and despair, victim and victimizer, dream and reality, pity and hatred, and friend and stranger helps define Boston's urban community as a site of contradictions and contested meaning.

Lefebvre's Triangle

While Jimmy embodies a passionate, if corrupt, notion of family values and Dave is a victim turned violent, Sean's role within the city is less easy to place. Sean is the only character without a distinct past reputation within "the old community", and since his childhood he has moved ostensibly to a newer and more expensive neighborhood. His urban anxieties do not have to do with centrifugal globalizing forces or the recovery of an innocent self. Instead, he expresses a general frustration in lamenting the hopelessness and depressing daily realities of crime within the city. Sean's immense emotional distance from the community and its desires is paralleled with his emotional and physical distance from his wife. What, then, is Sean's role within the Boston neighborhood? I argue that Sean is a carrier of abstract space. If we locate Sean's role within Lefebvre's triangle of representations of space, representational space, and spatial practices, he would belong to the category of representations of space, which is necessarily the space of planners and bureaucrats (McCann 1999, p. 171). He embodies a type of space that is conceived rather than lived. It is associated with perception rather than emotional embodiment and consists almost entirely of abstract space. In one of the final scenes in the film, Sean and Jimmy spot each other across the crowd while attending a neighborhood parade. Sean shapes his hand in the likeness of a gun, and points and metaphorically "shoots" Jimmy. This symbolic gesture refuses to grant the film a sense of closure or a definitive moral conclusion of its own. More importantly, it emphasizes the public, visible, and contradictory nature of the abstract space that Sean occupies throughout the film.

Since Sean is in the Homicide department of the state police, he is integral to the processes that control and bound space for the purposes of investigation. The abstract space that Sean inhabits represents the state, the law, and public spaces. Sean's workspace includes the state police office, public bridges, and Penitentiary Park, among other state jurisdictions, and in each instance, the space is largely insulated from any unauthorized users. Like all abstract space, the space he inhabits is largely homogeneous and is unmarked by signs of histories, which have been erased or forgotten (McCann 1999, p. 170). As I noted at the outset, Sean serves as a bridge character who brings together and mediates interactions between Jimmy and Dave, although it is the abstract space of the state rather than Sean's charisma that allows him to perform this mediating role. By constructing Sean as a mediator, I do not intend to imply neutrality; the statements and actions of the state police reinforce certain prejudices and boundaries within the city. Instead, Sean as a character embodies a kind of abstract space which

> can be seen ... as a continual struggle between the state and capital trying to produce and maintain a seemingly homogenous but fundamentally contradictory abstract space, on the one hand, and subaltern groups, often working through oppositional elements in the media, asserting their counter spaces and constructing their counter publics on the other. (McCann 1999, p. 180)

Examples of contestation between this abstract space and local, lived space include Jimmy's successful attempt to penetrate the blockade around Penitentiary Park surrounding the crime scene, as well as Dave's successful attempt to reverse the burden of proof onto the state department while being questioned by Whitey Powers at the state police office.

While this is evidence of the contradictions inherent in abstract space, Sean himself embodies some of these contradictions. For example, he claims objectivity and denies a conflict of interest in Katie Markum's case due to his previous friendship with both Jimmy and Dave. However, Sean tends to give Dave much more leeway during the investigation than does Whitey Powers. In addition, Sean does little or nothing to convict Jimmy, despite his knowledge that Jimmy murdered Dave. Sean is the only main character lacking a clear-cut childhood reputation, indicating his weaker ties to the "old neighborhood" and his ability to represent one who fled or escaped, though not entirely, the influences of the area he grew up in. Sean also mediates the way in which encounters are affectively portrayed; he does not embody pain in the same way that Jimmy and Dave do.

In the case of Dave's character, it is instructive to turn to Lauren Berlant's (2000, p. 56) definition of pain as a public form that makes one readable for others. When Dave escapes from the child molesters several days after his abduction, the community "reads" him as damaged goods. As a result, people withdraw emotional attachments so that sympathy towards him is limited, while their collective memory never fails to expunge the potential threat of the victim. Berlant's (2000, p. 49) recognition of the destabilizing effects of pain on the ability to represent it and the tendency for the agency of the subject to disappear and be transferred to the place is relevant to the representations of emotion in the film. In the case of Dave as victim, his agency is very much diminished in his own eyes as well as in the eyes of the community, and is transferred to various real and imagined places. Dave uses a vampire metaphor to describe the transfer of agency to an imaginary being — he schizophrenically describes the person who he has become as "[t]he boy who escaped from the wolves, [who] is no longer Dave" (Lehane 2001, p. 26). Sean Devine also describes a transfer of agency to another imaginary place, "death". When Jimmy asks Sean when the last time he saw Dave was, he responds: "That was twenty-five years ago, going up this street, in the back of that car". In Stuart Aitkin's (2006, p. 497) analysis of *Mystic River*, he rightly distinguishes the affective, visceral, and emotional encounters that we see mapped onto or inhabiting the bodies of the male characters in the film from other encounters that are subject to identity-fixing representations. It is apparent even with a cursory understanding of the plot that the identities of Jimmy and Dave are anything but stable, and this instability is affectively demonstrated (rather than represented) using uncomfortably intimate close-ups of their faces that reveal bodies marked with raw expressions of suffering and pain.

Jimmy's character stretches the ideas of contingencies and interdependence the farthest:

> If we got in that car, life would have been a very different thing ... And so we never would have had Katie. And Katie, then never would have been murdered. But she was. All because we didn't get in that car. (Lehane 2001, pp. 173-175)

By internalizing all the blame for Katie's murder, Jimmy in effect grants himself a great deal of agency; he equates his victimization to a personal responsibility for retribution. This is a case inasmuch as an act of mourning is effectively "an act of aggression and of social death making" (Berlant 2000, p. 43). Jimmy more or less claims a large amount of responsibility within the community, which allows for an "objective" and "just" assessment of all matters affecting him. It is Jimmy's true belief in the world view that living is the cause of death which makes him a romantic/tragic character. His defensive rhetoric veils blind revenge. After refusing to believe Dave's innocence in Katie's murder, he forces a fake confession and then stabs Dave in the stomach, all the while maintaining a sincerely pained and tortured visage: "We bury our sins here, Dave. We wash them clean" (Lehane 2001, p. 366).

If the fatalistic film noir genre is notorious for presenting a rationalized alienating system that offers no escape (Dimendberg 2004, p. 12), then the film's neo-noir variation on this theme offers instead a more banal, quotidian, and incidental inability to escape the neighborhood as well as one's own past. Sean had been largely successful at avoiding "the old neighborhood" and his old friends Jimmy and Dave until he was assigned to investigate the murder of Katie Markum as a State Homicide detective. How does this continuation of the past into the present and seeming inability to escape one's past convey what Bakhtin (1981, p. 37) terms a conflict within internal and external selves? While Jimmy's pain and suffering are embodied within or marked onto his body and displayed affectively or emotionally in the close-ups throughout the film, the descriptions within the novel describe his internal dilemma more precisely. There are narratives within the novel that are propelled by what Bakhtin calls "chronotopes", or matrixes which realize the interconnectedness of time and space: "I'm just saying there are threads, okay? Threads in our lives. You pull one, and everything else gets affected ... Say you and me, Sean, say we got in that car with Dave Boyle" (Lehane 2001, p. 155).

This recognition of contingencies and the leveling effects of time and space (expressed in Jimmy's remark) allows for this particular neighborhood of Boston to form an intimate and lasting relationship with its inhabitants. The Boston neighborhood, rather than the center of the city, serves as the basic stable unit of representation, thus taking on an autonomous quality. It is a domain worthy of pride, hate, and protection from infiltration. This conception of the partitioning of urban society focuses on the effects of centrifugal forces rather than centripetal forces. It attributes importance to the ways in which the urban is encroaching on the margins of the city, rather than expressing concern for extreme concentration at the center. It is fitting to turn to a novel to analyze the ways in which centrifugal forces are at work because, as Bakhtin suggests in the 'Discourse in the Novel' essay from his *The Dialogic Imagination* (1981), novels thrive on distinctions and rely on tensions between centrifugal and centripetal tendencies. Lefebvre further demonstrates that these tendencies can be manifested towards an urban effect: "unlike the post-industrial society, urban society refers to tendencies, orientations and virtualities rather than one pre-ordained reality" (Lefebvre 2003, p. 2). In this modern neo-noir portrayal of Boston in *Mystic River*, one does not get the sense that there is an unstoppable and heartless police state in the name of free enterprise and individuality. Instead, there are individuals whose choices reflect their own urban desires and anxieties. It is the often conflicting and necessarily heteroglossic nature of urban imaginaries and urban realities that can result in tragedy for individual characters. In the film version, the impact of tragedy is registered in close-ups of faces with pained expressions.

Aesthetics and Cinematic Production of Meaning

Elaine Scarry (1987, p. 13) discusses the difficulties inherent in attempts to represent pain, and the instrumental role of language in attempting to either "coax pain into visibility" or "push it into further invisibility". Here, I look at the ways in which the cinematic form coaxes pain into visibility for the viewer, and find that the inability to fully represent the pain embodied by the characters in *Mystic River* parallels the inability to fully represent the subject of the film — the peripheral neighborhood in South Boston. It is primarily an aesthetic engagement with the architecture and buildings, which serve as vehicles for representing the local lifeworld. The built environment performs as a character in the film — but with autonomy that exists outside of the plot. The scenes central to the advancement of the plot are interrupted frequently by shots depicting a dark and eerie Mystic River. The scenes featuring working-class Boston depict a vernacular architecture that is alienating and indifferent. Houses are often framed at a distance, and porches, stairs, and hallways are repetitively used as framing devices that seem to incarcerate those occupying the space by visually suggesting that it is structures themselves that restrict movement (see Figure 1).

The autonomy that belongs to the architecture and buildings themselves should be attributed to the vision of the film as a whole rather than the plot. The film's emphasis on subjects that eschew total representation results in implications that are political and ideological in nature rather than psychological. In the scene in which Jimmy Markum discovers that his daughter has been murdered, the camera zeroes in on Jimmy's tortured face. The yell that escapes him is ineffable. So

Figure 1 Jimmy Markum sits in close proximity to his soon-to-be victim Dave Boyle on his own front doorsteps in the fictional Boston neighborhood that is the focal point of the film *Mystic River*.

many scenes in the film use the same cinematic strategies to deal with violence and pain; yet without engaging a plot oriented toward emotional resolution because the film effectively displaces psychology with political sensibility. No possible solutions to personal problems are presented because "problems" are framed ideologically rather than psychologically.

As the film actively produces images that are suggestive of architecture's passive and uncaring role — streets and houses contribute little or nothing to those living in the neighborhood — we see a world in which space inhibits communitarian sentiment. Effectively, the angles of vision in the architectural shots in Eastwood's *Mystic River* are reminiscent of Pasolini's filming style in his *Mamma Roma* (1962), where Pasolini provides ideological rather than subjective images of Rome. Pasolini's aesthetic engagement with architecture in the peripheries of Rome necessarily "thrusts the viewer back into the realm of the political" (Rhodes 2007, p. 135), inviting critical thought that has implications which are much more ethical than they are psychological. Just as in *Mystic River*, this ideological surplus pervading *Mamma Roma* does not enrich the storyline but instead enhances the meaning of the film (Rhodes 2007, p. 127). The film itself can be said to contain a meaning of its own that relies heavily on the autonomous role of architecture. The meaning of the film is enhanced by ideological images in ways that the characters cannot fully understand. In *Mamma Roma*, a particular building is shot from a considerable distance, and similar shots occur frequently throughout the film, thereby establishing an autonomy of their own (Rhodes 2007, p. 113). In creating an indifferent architectural autonomy, both films create an anti-ideal city in which "the faculty of presentation, the imagination, fails to provide a representation corresponding to this Idea" (Rhodes 2007, p. 81). While attempts to represent the periphery are essential to the suffering that occurs, the weight of the suffering is placed entirely on the characters.

As I have mentioned earlier, there is an aesthetic advantage in the novel's ability to represent "the past as the past". However, cinema has its aesthetic advantages as well, especially the advantage of being a decentered or centerless mode of meaning creation. Both *Mamma Roma* and *Mystic River* engage in the process of unperceiving; through their concrete depictions, they restore what perception tends to evacuate. Each film's aesthetic orientation — its way of mobilizing images — resists the dominant modes of world-making and serves to encourage the viewer to think. Indeed, the films themselves think in ways that disrupt or blur existing modes of representation. Pasolini's film suggests "a modernism that is engaged in blurring the boundaries between modernism and its binary others" (Rhodes 2007, p. 77). The blurring of boundaries in both cases involves applying criticisms of the urban center to the periphery. *Mamma Roma* applies the aesthetic principles of the Roman Romantic — immensity, confusion, ineffability — to the Roman periphery (Rhodes 2007, p. 83). As Deleuze would have it, this use of space and positionality in the cinema "deprivileges the directionality of centered commanding perception; it allows the disorganized multiplicity that is the world to emerge" (Shapiro in press). *Mystic River* similarly displaces a violent cartography often associated with urban centers with a more removed South Boston neighborhood. In both cases — Pasolini's *Mamma Roma* and Eastwood's *Mystic River* — it is primarily the *mise en scène* rather than the storyline that conveys a violent cartography alongside a timeless landscape. Thus, in *Mystic River*, as in *Mamma Roma*, it is through the production of images rather than through its primary narrative thrust that the film thinks; action images are trumped by perception images. The perceptual limitations of the characters are juxtaposed with what the viewers are encouraged to discern as the films' moving images articulation of the contexts of suffering embodied in the characters — mainly Jimmy Markum and Dave Boyle in *Mystic River*, as is the case with Mamma Roma in the film of the same name.

References

Aitkin, S. (2006) 'Leading Men to Violence and Creating Spaces for Their Emotions', *Gender, Place and Culture*, vol. 13, no. 5, pp. 491–507.

Bakhtin, M. M. (1981) *The Dialogic Imagination*, University of Texas Press, Austin, TX.

Bergson, H. (1990) *Matter and Memory*, trans. Paul, N. M. and Palmer, W. S., Zone Books, New York.

Berlant, L. (2000) 'The Subject of True Feeling: Pain, Privacy, and Politics', in Dean, J. (ed.), *Cultural Studies and Political Theory*, Cornell University Press, Ithaca, NY.
Burch, N. (1995) *Theory of Film Practice*, trans. Lane, H., Praeger Publishers, New York.
Dimendberg, E. (2004) *Film Noir and the Spaces of Modernity*, Harvard University Press, Cambridge, MA.
Highmore, B. (2005) *Cityscapes: Cultural Readings in the Material and Symbolic City*, Palgrave Macmillan, New York.
Krause, L. & Petro, P. (eds) (2003) *Global Cities: Cinema, Architecture, and Urbanism in a Digital Age*, Rutgers University Press, New Brunswick, NJ.
Lasswell, H. D. (1977) *Psychopathology and Politics*, University of Chicago Press, Chicago, IL.
Lefebvre, H. (2003) *The Urban Revolution*, trans. Bononno, R., University of Minnesota Press, Minneapolis, MN.
Lehane, D. (2001) *Mystic River*, Harper Collins, New York.
McCann, E. (1999) 'Race, Protest, and Public Space: Contextualizing Lefebvre in the U.S City', *Antipode*, vol. 31, no. 2, pp. 163-184.
Mumford, L. (1961) *The City in History: Its Origins, Its Transformations, and Its Prospects*, Harvest Books, San Diego, CA.
Mystic River (2003) dir. Clint Eastwood, Warner Bros. Pictures, USA.
Rhodes, J. D. (2007) *Stupendous Miserable City*, University of Minnesota Press, Minneapolis, MN.
Sanders, J. (2003) *Celluloid Skyline: New York and the Movies*, Alfred A. Knopf, New York.
Scarry, E. (1987) *The Body in Pain: The Making and Unmaking of the World*, Oxford University Press, New York.
Shapiro, M. (in press) *Cinematic Geopolitics (Global Horizons)*, Routledge, London.
They Shoot Pictures, Don't They?, http://www.theyshootpictures.com/eisensteinsergei.htm.

Intercity Cinema: Hong Kong at the Berlinale

Michael J. Shapiro

This article is an analysis of Yau Nai-Hoi's film *Eye in the Sky*, a detective thriller set in present-day Hong Kong, which was viewed at the 2007 Berlin Film Festival. The article is situated by the author's experience of viewing. Just as the author was continuously involved in timing his movements within the rush of the city of Berlin, one of the film's main protagonists, the head of a theft ring, was also busy timing Hong Kong's movements. The author's film experience thus involved movement from one fraught temporal habitus to another. In addition, both the city that was the locus of the author's viewing and the city of the film are newly reconfigured. Berlin, now a unified national capital after a significant political reorientation, is full of large corporate and government buildings as well as large consumption emporiums in places that were once quite different. And Berlin's reconfiguration, like Hong Kong's, has taken place in a highly politicized context — in Berlin's case, an attempt at an architecture of civil society, of public space and of "democratic transparency", in order to reorient the problem of Germanness, while Hong Kong is also involved in an identity problematic, its relationship with Chineseness.

From the start, the city was the natural backdrop for film. (Wesemann 2000, p. 31)

Multiple temporalities coexist in urban space. (King 2006, p. 16)

Introduction: Peripatetic Film Viewing

Berlin, February 2007: as an attendee at the 2007 Berlin Film Festival (the Berlinale), I was a cinema-focused tourist, negotiating both a larger and smaller space in a complex urban venue. Occasionally on public transportation but mostly on foot in the city, I became what Walter Benjamin (1968, p. 175) famously refers to as "a *kaleidoscope* equipped with consciousness"; I was functioning with the kind of fragmented perceptual apparatus that reflects the shocks delivered by the city's fragmented, hyperstimulating environment.[1] As

---

1. I am indebted to my friend and colleague Konrad Ng, a frequent festival attendee, for helping me manage my Berlinale experience.

Benjamin (ibid.) notes, such shocks are also delivered by film, which formalizes the shocks of the city's sensorium. First, I was situated in Berlin as a whole, a city that no longer conformed to its expected imaginary because its recent reconstruction had effaced most of its Cold War history. Gone was the Berlin Wall as well as much of what else had been the cityscape around Potsdamer Platz, the main festival site. That city center, which had once been in the eastern sector of the formerly divided Berlin, and for years since had been primarily a construction site, is now a thriving commercial center with theaters, shops, and restaurants, enframed in an architecture that is reminiscent of the Potsdamer Platz of the 1920s and '30s — a busy square that serves as "a major transport hub ... and contain[s] numerous bars, cafes and cinemas" but owes nothing to its recent past.[2] The recent historical instability of Berlin's built environment is paralleled by "a certain fragility of national identity" (Guy 2004, p. 77) owed largely to a past from which Berliners, like most contemporary Germans, would like to distance themselves. At the same time Berliners are engaged in a "proliferation of, and struggle over, alternative futures" (ibid.).

Second, I was also situated in a smaller version of the city, the "cinematic heterotopia" that the Berlinale creates for 10 days every year, consisting of a film center that houses the marketing displays, an information and ticket center where festival attendees queue to register and obtain film tickets, several designated theaters for the screenings, and a few shuttle vehicles that run between the film center and the other Berlinale venues.[3] Both spaces — the larger city and the smaller cinematic version — imposed timing and coping demands. Initially, there was a need to manage the bus, U-Bahn (subway), and S-Bahn (metro railway) routes, first to get to my hotel, and thereafter, as the days of my attendance transpired, to match the film administration and theater map with my city map, in order to secure my film attendance preferences and get to the theaters. There is a theoretically pregnant homology between my experience of Berlin and my cinema spectatorship. My travel around the city, involved in what Giuliana Bruno calls "site-seeing", articulated smoothly with my film viewing. Inasmuch as cinema enacts moving spaces, film viewing is a "kinetic affair" with a striking similarity to what is experienced in street walking (Bruno 2002, pp. 15-17). To move from the city streets into the theater, a shift from *voyageur* to *voyeur*, is thus to enact a transition from one kinetic experience to another.

For purposes of the cinematic event that provides the primary material for this analysis, a Hong Kong film, the locus of my film viewing connected a mobile consumption of Berlin with an experience of a cinematically dynamic Hong Kong. Moreover, my viewing experiences were targeted on two cities that have been

---

2. The quotation is from a website on the history of the Potsdamer Platz. See http://aviewoncities.com/berlin/potsdamerplatz.htm (accessed 11 March 2007).

3. The expression 'cinematic heterotopia' belongs to Victor Burgin (2004, p. 7). As a heterotopia, or space of otherness, the Berlinale is constituted as a space from which to reflect on the typical spaces of the urban. As Foucault, who created the concept, notes, the value of a 'heterotopia' is the extent to which its separation from ordinary spaces affords one the possibility of reflection on the ordering effects of space (Foucault 1986).

scenes of dramatic transfer (with attendant identity consequences) — the transfer of the capital from Bonn to Berlin and the transfer of Hong Kong from Britain's to China's control. Effectively, in the transition from the Potsdamer Platz of the new German capital to a theater with a film treating the recently transferred Hong Kong, I was moving from one recently reoriented city square to another; "the screen", as Paul Virilio (1991, p. 25) puts it, has become "since the beginning of the twentieth century ... the city square". While certainly the dramas of the two cities' histories inflect the inter-articulation of walking and viewing, the management of two examples of dense of urban stimuli has the effect of foregrounding urban erotics as well. As Roland Barthes, who also addressed the effects of movement from the city streets to the film theater, puts it: "The movie auditorium condenses the 'modern eroticism' of the big city".[4]

Two aspects of history introduce temporal imaginaries that compete with the "eroticism" of my cinematic experience. There is both a cinema history which impinges on film viewing in Berlin and a geopolitical history that haunts contemporary Berlin. With respect to the former, in consuming cinema in Berlin, one is participating in a historical trajectory of a city—cinema articulation in which Berlin has famously participated from early in the twentieth century. The pioneering cinematic treatments of Berlin are Walter Ruttmann's *Berlin: The Symphony of a Great City* (1927) and Dziga Vertov's *Man with a Movie Camera* (1929). As those films indicate, from early in its development in Berlin (as in other cities), cinema displayed "a structural affinity" with the city. As "a darkened chamber typically located at the heart of the big city [it] provided the space where modernity negotiated and tried to come to terms with its contradictory impulses of repression and revelation, transparency and obscurity" (Strathhausen 2003, p. 17). However, for me, the transitions from street to theater at the Berlinale were only smoothly articulated sensually and conceptually. As a bottom-feeder at the festival (one with access only to those films shown to the mass of attendees and not to those films restricted to persons with media and/or marketing credentials), I was moving about in a temporary "society of control", where access is regulated by codes (Deleuze 1992). The barcode on the badge I received when I registered allowed me to obtain the program booklet. Thereafter, it had to be scanned, both when I sought to obtain tickets and when I entered the theaters. On the one hand, the divided Berlin of the Cold War had been constituted pervasively as a society of control, and aspects of that former control remain part of Berlin's geopolitical framing. Reflecting this irrepressible past that still marks the city, close to the main festival sites was the famous Cold War barrier between the east and west sectors of the city, Checkpoint Charlie, now a preserved space of historical memory that is open to all as a tourist site. On the other hand, there were the Berlinale checkpoints, which distinguished the eligible from the non-eligible for each film.

---

4. The Barthes quotation, from his *The Pleasure of the Text* (1973), is taken from Burgin (2004, p. 34), who elaborates this Barthean conception.

Importantly, this dual spatiality I was negotiating — one with vestiges of a former control and one with temporarily implemented controls — was articulated with a dual temporality; the historical city of Berlin, which had been recently (and radically) transfigured, primarily to effect an overcoding of Germany's wars (both hot and cold), contained a brief cinematic event. In a space with a long temporal trajectory, which challenged my historical imagination, I had not only to appreciate the historical depth of city sites but also to focus on the short-term timing of my movements: rising and breakfasting early enough to avoid long lines at ticket counters (where one's only chance for a ticket required an appearance at least 48 hours ahead of the film's showing) and then showing up early enough to get a preferred seating section in the theater. At the same time, I was also consuming the historical city, timing both public transportation as well as festival-connected shuttles to move about the city in order to eat, shop, and visit such cultural sites as the Neue Nationalgalerie, which helped me become acquainted with aspects of Berlin's past.

This particular site turned out to provide a resource for my reflections on the relationship between the historic space of the city and the temporary space of the festival, as well as on the identity differences between Berlin and Hong Kong. Roaming through the art museum's exhibition rooms, I encountered Ernst Ludwig Kirchner's (1914) eponymous painting of an early version of the Potsdamer Platz (see Figure 1). I had been wondering how that city center, now fundamentally redesigned and rebuilt so that it is dominated by large emporiums of consumption — for example, the new, massive Sony Center — must affect those who remember both the pre-war and Cold War versions. Kirchner created an image of the place as it must have been experienced by residents and visitors in the early part of the twentieth century. His rendering of the Potsdamer Platz captures an essential experience of modern urban life, while at the same time resonating with my city and festival experiences. The bodies in the Platz manifest the typical kinetic energy of city-dwellers in motion. There are various elegantly attired pedestrians in close proximity and in brisk walking postures. Their positioning and directional orientations display a studied indifference to each other. Even the two women in the foreground, in very close proximity and caught in mid stride on a circular pedestal-like section of pavement, are oriented obliquely to each other.

Kirchner's style captures two aspects of modern life. First, the kinetic energy in his urban paintings anticipates the cinema—city relationship. Like Ruttmann and Vertov, whose documentaries captured Berlin's dynamism, Kirchner's Berlin scenes reflect the hyperkinetic feeling that the city conveyed to him. As he put it (speaking about himself in the third person):

> He discovered that the feeling that pervades a city presented itself in the qualities of the lines of force (*Kraftlinien*). In the way in which groups of persons configured themselves in the rush, in the trams, how they moved, this is how he discovered the means to capture what he had experienced.[5]

5. The quotation is a translation from Kirchner's diary (*Tagebuch*) quoted in Haxthausen (1990, p. 67).

Figure 1 Kirchner's *Potsdamer Platz* (1914).

Second, Kirchner's rendering remains contemporary. Despite massive changes in the configuration of the Potsdamer Platz, the essential urban demands of the Berlin of the early twentieth century remain in force in the early twenty-first. Contemporary Berlin, like other urban venues, continues to require an effort at interpersonal indifference in situations of close interpersonal proximity.

Given the cinematic quality of Berlin's moving energy and the need for one to manage its temporal rhythms while maintaining the posture of an indifference-in-close-proximity that belongs to city-dwellers, the city habitus of my film viewing was like the situation in the opening scene of the film that most captured my attention at the festival, Yau Nai-Hoi's *Eye in the Sky*, a detective thriller set in present-day Hong Kong. Just as I was continuously involved in timing my movements within the rush of the city, one of the film's main protagonists, the head of a theft ring, was also busy timing Hong Kong's movements. My film experience thus involved movement from one fraught temporal habitus to another. In addition, both the city that was the locus of my viewing and the city of the film are newly reconfigured. Berlin, now a unified national capital after a significant political reorientation, is full of large corporate and government buildings as well as large consumption emporiums in places that were once quite different. And Berlin's reconfiguration, like Hong Kong's, has taken place in a highly politicized context — in Berlin's case, an attempt at "an architecture of civil society", of "public space" and of "democratic transparency" (Kramer 1999, p. 57). The architecture of the new Berlin faced the issue of "how to make a credible Berlin out of a city with no consensual idea of itself and no common history beyond a negative one" (Kramer 1999, p. 58). Among other things, to efface the Berlin imaginary of Hitler's architect — Albert Speer's Berlin design — the government sector runs on an east—west axis, in opposition to the north—south orientation envisioned by Speer (Wise 1999).

The political problematic surrounding the creation of the new Hong Kong involved a different kind of erasure. Hong Kong's transition was a movement from a colonially controlled "emporium" to a modern (still colonial) global city. It was, in Ackbar Abbas's (1999, pp. 294-295) terms, a movement to a "colonial space of disappearance", where "disappearance" is intrinsic to contemporary culture insofar as Hong Kong culture defies the traditional binaries — for example East—West — through which it has been historically represented. Shaped by the "long goodbye" to British control and the preparation for mainland China's reclaiming of the city state, Hong Kong's architecture is a combination of the old and the new. As a perennial "intersection of spaces" with a long history of a changing ethnoscape as well as changing loci of power and control, Hong Kong has had a "floating identity", which articulates well with its fluvial situation (Abbas 1997, pp. 3-4). As one commentator on Abbas's insight aptly puts it:

> The local is experienced as a field of instability, discontinuity, and exclusiveness that transforms any available models of culture ... This elusive, translated local can come to presence, paradoxically, only when it is going to become extinct with the possible disappearance of its former lifestyle after the 1997 handover. (Lo 2005, p. 99)

One aspect of Hong Kong's local culture that speaks to this paradox is enacted in the film *Chicken and Duck Talk* (1988), produced by Ronnie Yu and directed by Clifton Ko. The film narrative treats the threat to a traditional local restaurant run by Danny Poon of expanding global food franchises such as McDonalds and Kentucky Fried Chicken, which are in close proximity to his establishment. Animating a classic story (originally in novel form) that "portrays a post-traditional Hong Kong where established cultural values are challenged by market logic" (Stokes & Hoover 1999, p. 174), the film expresses an aspect of Hong Kong food culture precisely at a moment when it is threatened with disappearance. Sharon Zukin captures the tensions involved in Hong Kong's encounter between cultural commitments and economic forces:

> [A] postmodern urban landscape not only maps culture and power; it also maps the opposition between *markets* — the economic forces that detach people from established social institutions — and *place* — the spatial forms that anchor them to the social world, providing the basis of a stable identity. (Zukin 1992, p. 223)

It should be noted that across the range of cultural modalities, what is threatened with disappearance is relatively recent. It was not until the mid-1960s that

"Hong Kong's historically migrant society harbored a majority native-born population" (Fang 2003, p. 297). What is local or native, and thus what is "Hong Kong culture", has a short historical trajectory, even though much of Hong Kong culture partakes, in varying degrees, of southern Chinese culture. The instability of Hong Kong's ethnoscape and cultural practices is paralleled by its architecture. Hong Kong's "architecture of disappearance" (Abbas 1997, p. 66) defies a history of representational binaries applied to the city state because the city combines sites of selective cultural preservation — for example, "the Hong Kong Cultural Center on the site of the old Hong Kong railway terminal" (ibid.) — along with culturally indistinguishable structures — for example, signature buildings by architects with global credentials (among other things, like Berlin, Hong Kong has a new I. M. Pei building). Most significantly, for purposes of this analysis, Hong Kong cinema articulates Hong Kong's complex spatial history, emphasizing a variety of scopic regimes from alternative perspectives. In general, as Abbas (1997, pp. 16-17) has pointed out, Hong Kong cinema has responded to the "space of disappearance", articulated as an intersection of imperialism and globalism, with images and narratives that explore that conflicted space. More specifically, contemporary Hong Kong cinema reflects a spatial history through the ways in which it focuses alternatively on the city's vernacular and global architectures (Abbas 1999, p. 308).

Yau's *Eye in the Sky*

In the case of Yau's *Eye in the Sky*, what is articulated as a set of scopic regimes are two systems of surveillance, enacted by a theft ring on the one hand and the Investigative Bureau (IB) of the Hong Kong police on the other, both set within the spaces and temporal rhythms of the city. The film's opening displays the more venerable aspects of the urban experience captured in Kirchner's painting of Berlin's Potsdamer Platz — the demand for indifference in the face of crowded proximity. *Eye in the Sky* begins with a vertical panning shot of the new Hong Kong, followed by an exposure of the frenetic pace of a modern global city. The first shot is a vertical pan, aimed initially at tall buildings and then slowly descending toward the street, where the focus is on moving traffic. The camera then zooms in on a bus, which stops to pick up a man, whom we later learn is Chan Chong Shan (Tony Leung), the head of a theft ring.

After this initial sequence, the opening scene proceeds with a striking resemblance to Samuel Fuller's classic Cold War noir thriller *Pickup on South Street* (1953), which begins with an exterior shot of a moving subway in New York and then takes the viewer inside, where a typical urban transportation scenario is evident. All the passengers on the New York subway, including the protagonists — a federal agent, Zara (Willis B. Bouchey), a police captain, Dan Tiger (Murvyn Vye), and their suspect, "Candy" (Jean Peters), whom they think is giving military intelligence to communists — maintain a feigned indifference to their fellow riders, even though some of them are intimately connected (which becomes

Figure 2 Candy and McCoy on the subway in *Pickup on South Street* (1953).

evident later in the film narrative) (see Figure 2). Their studied air of distraction is underscored when a pickpocket, Skip McCoy (Richard Widmark), manages to steal Candy's wallet with no one noticing until the theft is accomplished. Zara and Tiger rush toward the closing doors, too late to pursue McCoy.

The scene on the Hong Kong bus mimics Fuller's scene. Chan Chong Shan takes a seat next to an attractive young woman, an undercover constable Ho Ka-Po/"Piggy" (Kate Tsui), who, it turns out, is involved in crime-surveillance training. They avoid eye contact as Shan proceeds to don his glasses and work on a Sudoku puzzle book, while (code name) Piggy closes her eyes momentarily and appears to be concentrating on the music from an iPod plugged into one ear (see Figure 3). She steals a glance at a man feigning sleep several seats away and across from her. He turns out to be Sergeant Wong Man Chin/"Dog Head" (Simon Yam), her undercover police surveillance mentor, who is tailing her to evaluate her competence. Thus, *Eye in the Sky*'s opening scene, like *Pickup on South Street*'s, introduces the viewer not only to the main protagonists but also to a typical urban *mise en scène* — people moving about the city in crowded proximity, while maintaining an air of mannered indifference to each other.

The two films' surveillance regimes, operating within different historical—political frames and venues, hark back to the initial literature of detection,

GENRE AND THE CITY

Figure 3 Shan and Piggy on the bus in *Eye in the Sky*.

which emerged in the nineteenth century along with the "immense human traffic of the centripetal metropolis" (Dimendberg 2004, p. 25). But their storylines treat different problematics. While the political frame in *Pickup on South Street* involves the vagaries of the anti-communist hysteria of the 1950s, the micropolitics of crime that frames *Eye in the Sky* emerges from attention to the forces shaping the rapidly changing post-colonial Hong Kong, which has become a global city dominated by the banking, accounting, and legal services, along with the commerce that characterizes such cities. While the images in *Eye in the Sky* eventually capture those forces, the film's narrative progression, following from the scene on the bus, articulates the beginning of one of the film's narrative threads — a becoming professional of a new recruit, a genre known as the *roman d'éducation*. Constable Ho Ka-Po, aka "Piggy", is learning to be an effective detective. After the three principals — Shan, Piggy, and Dog Head — leave the bus, all seemingly headed in different directions, Piggy ends up in a restaurant, where Dog Head also enters after surreptitiously following her through the streets. Piggy and Dog Head's eventual quarry, Shan, heads in precisely the opposite direction from Dog Head, after leaving the bus directly behind him. He walks through the city as the camera tracks the kinetics of moving pedestrian traffic on the sidewalks and vehicular traffic on the streets. He then moves through a shopping arcade, past some upscale shops, and finally up a ramp that affords a high perch from which he prepares his surveillance of the local scene around the jewelry store that his gang is about to rob.

At this point, the film narrative proceeds within what David Bordwell (2002, p. 89) identifies as a "forking-path plot", a film narrative that "proceeds from a fixed point" (in this case the stop at which the protagonists leave the bus) and heads off in "mutually exclusive lines of action". However, while Shan heads off to manage a robbery and Piggy and Dog Head proceed in a different direction for a rendezvous in connection with their policing vocation, their paths will ultimately intersect, as is the case with many "forking-path plots, because the cohesion of such plots are appointments", for example, deaths or other forms of consummation (Bordwell 2002, p. 94). In *Eye in the Sky*, the intersection of the paths will come when Piggy's path leads to Shan's capture and killing. Shan's catastrophe at this intersection also involves a competence issue, in his case the incompetence of some of his gang members, who violate Shan's timing codes because they cannot defer gratification.

Significantly, therefore, what drives the two paths or action trajectories are professional commitments — one kind that succeeds (the police's) and another that fails (the gang members'). And, crucially, bearing in mind the complexities that constitute Hong Kong's unusual historical situation, the two sets of commitments reflect much of the way the film articulates Hong Kong's micropolitical forces. Vocational commitments are unusually strong forms of allegiance in a city that has had an unstable civic identity and solicits little by way of national allegiance. As a result, vocational allegiance has more identity weight than it might have in places where national and civic allegiances have strong effectivity. Indeed, in the case of Hong Kong, the policing vocation has been unusually important from the colonial to the post-colonial period. As one history of Hong Kong policing observes: "the Hong Kong police survive as guardians of the territories' political stability and cultural identity" (Fang 2003, p. 293). In addition, inasmuch as Hong Kong is effectively a city state, the policing identity has special cultural authority because it "also doubles as national defense" (Fang 2003, p. 303). Moreover, as is evident in the film, the policing establishment is now on the cutting edge of technical sophistication. As Karen Fang (2003, p. 301) puts it: "Their ubiquitous officers, vehicles, technological devices, and architectural sites ... represent their postcolonial authority."

To return to Shan's path after he leaves the bus, this is a point at which the film articulates well with the regimen of my Berlinale experience. Shan's task at this juncture in the film narrative is one of timing the rhythms of the city to manage an event. At the point at which his men arrive in a car, mask their faces, and enter the store, Shan sets his stopwatch to three minutes and begins scrutinizing the area around the store, while the camera swings around, showing two of his assistants, who survey the surroundings from street level. However, while a dramatic event, a jewelry store robbery, activates the rest of the film narrative, much of the film's focus and significance is a non-narrative treatment of modern Hong Kong's lifeworld. In this sense, Yau's *Eye in the Sky* conforms to what Jacques Rancière (2004, p. 24) refers to as the contemporary "aesthetic regime of the arts", which abandons "the primacy of the narrative over the descriptions" and employs "a fragmented or proximate mode of focalization, which imposes raw presence to the detriment of the rational sequences of the story".

Apart from the "forking-path plot" in which the film's drama is activated, two persistent images of contemporary Hong Kong constitute the primary descriptive gloss on the city early in the film, both based on the ways in which Hong Kong is saturated with modern technologies. Although Shan's stopwatch is the only visible piece of technology involved in the robbery (apart from his gang's weapons), it is evident that the gang has also used a mapping and timing of city traffic. Among other things, a truck, which followed the robbers' car, is used to block the road at the moment when the robbers emerge from the store and jump in their car to make their escape. At the same time that the robbery is in progress, Dog Head and Piggy make use of cell phones, and once they have connected in the restaurant and Dog Head has allowed Piggy to pass her test and become a detective (after closely questioning her on the details of what she has witnessed on the bus and thereafter), they arrive at the police station. There, Piggy is introduced to her new colleagues, but the interpersonal encounters appear less significant than the technological displays — advanced computer and video-feed technologies used to survey the city.

The film's shots enhance the surveillance thematic by emphasizing the densely saturated surveillance environment of Hong Kong. As the Shan gang's robbery is developing, the camera occasionally pans upward to show surveillance cameras both on the street, aimed at pedestrian and vehicular traffic, and in stores, aimed at customers. And some of the shots of the characters simulate the lenses of surveillance cameras. As the film cuts back and forth between the robbery dynamic and the education and professionalization of Piggy, the viewer is introduced to the vagaries of the two intimately connected vocations, crime and policing. The characters within both of these inter-articulated milieus are shown sharing two aspects of their respective practices, which are often in tension with each other — eating and surveillance. Indeed, eating in the cases of both the policing and crime personnel (on which the camera focuses frequently throughout the film) turns out to compete with the primary aspects of their vocational tasks.

The pervasive scenes of eating, at all times of the day and night, reflect the singular nature of Hong Kong's culinary culture. Once Dog Head finishes eating in the restaurant where he and Piggy first meet, they enter the police station, which is abuzz with news of the robbery, as various department personnel involve themselves with computers and surveillance videos. But the process of viewing and information sharing is momentarily suspended while one of the heads of the crime unit pauses to eat his soup, after announcing that it is "time for soup". Meanwhile, one of the Shan gang, "Fat Man", whose job it is to survey the street and watch out for police, is shown eating continuously. The first shots of Fat Man show him eating food off a skewer as he stands in a strategic position in the street outside the jewelry store. Then, at a crucial moment during the robbery, he looks through the window of a 7-Eleven convenience store and sees a man eating chicken off a bone, which he has obviously purchased within the store. Impulsively, Fat Man rushes into the store and buys a piece of chicken. And, tellingly, a surveillance camera records him swiping his "octopus card" (a card available from vending machines that can be used for transportation and small purchases throughout the city) to make the purchase. That sequence, which later helps the police to identify Fat Man as part of the robbery, reflects two aspects of Hong Kong, one singular and one shared with all modern cities.

First, let us look at the shared dimension. As William Leach has suggested, three technologies have combined historically to provoke consumer desire — color, glass, and light. Leach quotes from an advertising trade journal *Signs of the Times*, which speaks to the intended effects of the century-long development of the pervasive store windows and neon signs which Yau's camera focuses on continually: "Electrical advertising is a *picture medium*. Moreover it is a *color medium*; still again, electrical advertising is a medium of motion, of action, *of life, of light*, of compulsory attraction" (Leach 1993, p. 47). He goes on to note the way in which those technologies, incorporated into the modern store, effectively divided consumer classes in the early twentieth-century American city (and it applies well to contemporary Hong Kong, with its upscale stores on the one hand and its open market stalls on the other):

> Reliance on glass for display had several significant consequences: it contributed to the formation of a new culture of class — that is, it helped to demarcate more clearly the affluent from the poorer buying public ... Glass also closed off smell and touch, diminishing the consumer's relationship with the goods. At the same time it amplified the visual, transforming the already watching city person into a potentially compulsive viewer. (Leach 1993, pp. 62-63)

Fat Man's capitulation to an eating impulse at a crucial moment during the robbery articulates the summons that technologies have participated in for over a century all over the globe with something singular about Hong Kong's culinary culture. Certainly, the provocation of eating impulses is endemic to the modern city, which has witnessed "the penetration of food services into almost every other leisure site" (Bell & Valentine 1997, p. 130). But continual eating, at all hours and often while standing and walking, is more culturally specific. Although it is not wholly peculiar to Hong Kong, it is very much a Hong Kong cultural signature. A brief comparison with the culinary culture of Italy should suffice to highlight what is characteristic of Hong Kong eating practices. Donna Leon captures the Italian culinary habitus well in her Venice crime stories. For example, in her *Wilful Behaviour*, her perennial main character, police commissioner Guido Brunetti, engages in highly scheduled, elaborate, and slowly savored meals. At one point, "a little before twelve", she has him "beginning to think longingly of lunch" (Leon 2002, p. 13), and when he finally makes his way home for lunch (as is his habit throughout the stories in which he is featured), he sits down to a very elaborate repast, prepared by his wife Paola:

> In keeping with the changing season, Paola had risotto di zucca and into it at the last minute had tossed grated slivers of ginger, its sharp bite softened to amiability by the chunk of butter and the grated Parmigiano that had chased it into the pot. The mingled tastes drove all dread of Raffi's music [his son's annoying compact disc] from Brunetti's mind, and the chicken breast grilled with sage and white wine that followed replaced that music with what Brunetti thought must be the sound of angels singing. (Leon 2002, p. 66)

Brunetti drinks Chardonnay with the meal and follows his main course with a Braeburn apple and a thin slice of Montasio cheese, accompanied by a glass of Calvados (Leon 2002, p. 66).

In contrast to the timing and savoring central to the Italian culinary culture, Hong Kong eating, which is pervasively shown in Hong Kong films, is rapid and virtually continuous, in keeping with the frenetic pace of other dimensions of an urban lifeworld in which temporal boundaries hardly exist: for example, "the bright light of Hong Kong at night" can be "contrasted with rural China where evenings [are] covered with darkness" (Ma 2001, p. 447). In addition, food consumption in Hong Kong film tends to stand in for desire, *tout court*. For example, in Wong Kar-Wai's *Chungking Express* (1994), Eros is radically entangled with eating, as expressed in the sound track when Dinah Washington sings "It's heaven when you find romance on your menu".[6] In *Eye in the Sky*, one of the most significant eating scenes takes place at the theft ring's warehouse hideout. The robbery has seemingly succeeded, despite a violation of Shan's three-minute robbery model. One of the men tarried because, as he puts it, "I wanted more". The interference of his desire for more loot, like Fat Man's food lust, threatened the enterprise. Shan points this out and admonishes his head man for not controlling the maverick thief, who delayed their exit from the store. At this point, a furious fight breaks out, and Shan grabs a meat skewer and holds it to the maverick's throat.

The close-up camera shot of the skewer at the throat is not its first appearance. It is shown earlier — also with a close-up shot — as it is being used to impale a chicken part about to be barbecued. The skewer's dual iconic role becomes evident as the scene develops. After the argument and fight break up, one of the men looks out the window and notices an attractive young woman removing her clothes while standing near her window, in full view from the gang's point of observation. The viewer calls attention to the scene for the rest of the gang. They all stare, while the camera cuts back and forth between the decreasingly dressed figure of the woman and the rapt faces of the voyeurs, until the mood and focus is suddenly aborted as one of the men shouts, "Let's barbecue!" At this point, the skewer is once again returned to its primary purpose. Seemingly, the moment of erotic desire has been displaced by food consumption. However, more significantly, the sequence foregrounds the pervasive tension that Hong Kong shares with other cities in which distracting stimuli and possibilities for

---

6. I owe the specific reference to this film to David Bordwell's (2000) discussion in his chapter 'Romance on Your Menu' in *Planet Hong Kong*.

consumption are readily available. Shan, like the police officials in Hong Kong's IB, has to manage group tasks in the face of desire-provoking distractions. Both groups must pit codes against desire — policing codes on the one hand, which Dog Head incessantly imparts to Piggy, and robbery process codes on the other, which Shan attempts to impose on his gang as a whole.

While the two fraught pedagogies are unfolding in parallel, as the film cuts back and forth between them, the film's *mise en scène* is thinking well beyond the normative codes that organize the tasks of the two groups. By the time the second heist is about to go down, Shan discerns — again from a high perch overlooking the targeted jewelry store — that the police are closing in. He begins as usual by setting his watch, but he ultimately aborts the robbery and begins to evade the police, rushing away from his perch on foot. It becomes increasingly apparent, if we heed not only the close timing required for robberies but also the time images that operate as the framing of Hong Kong as a whole, that the city incorporates many layers of time which, for the viewer, emerge through the operation of "cinematic time", a mode of temporality that highlights the contingencies of encounter (Doane 2002). From the point of view of the cops and robbers thematic, which carries the film's dramatic narrative, the time issues are specific to managing robberies successfully on the one hand and to catching the culprits on the other. And both must be managed while competing with the temporal rhythms of bodily demands (both groups are shown perpetually eating, mostly rapidly, so as to interfere as little as possible with their vocational commitments). Within these task-related temporal problematics, what must be timed are the dynamics of entering and leaving a jewelry store, the intervals of police surveillance in the vicinity of the robberies, and the interval between the police being alerted to a robbery and their convergence on the scene. While timing issues of the robbery and the IB's attempts at apprehension are shown with cuts back and forth between the two groups, there are other ways in which the filming provides deeper levels of historical time.

Hong Kong historical time is conveyed with time images, which are interspersed between the drama, conveyed with action or movement images.[7] The initial time images are enacted with vertical panning shots, which are introduced before robberies, and also before each mobilization and pursuit by the IB policing unit. These vertical panning shots of the tall buildings deliver up the new, modern Hong Kong, in which much of the architecture reflects the differential prosperity of those who profit from the city's status as a key node in global exchanges.[8] However, when Shan makes his escape on foot through the city, and when Dog Head, Piggy, and the rest of the team fan out through the city on foot

---

7. The time images in Yau's film are not simply the indirect aspects of time that result from what Deleuze (1986) refers to as 'action-images'; there are often direct time images or 'chronosigns' in the film, which derive from the mode of time consciousness created by the camera's director-imposed mode of narration (see Deleuze 1989).

8. In Peter Taylor's (2000, p. 21) analysis of the key services provided by 'world cities' in the age of globalization, Hong Kong scores very high (only below New York and London) when total services scores on accountancy, banking/finance, and law are summed.

and in an unmarked van, the framing, tracking, and panning shots — all within a street-level, horizontal plane — deliver up a vernacular Hong Kong, in which local stores, street venders, and open-market enterprises exist alongside the more posh, global franchises that are targeted by criminal gangs.

Significantly, the Hong Kong that was leased to Britain for 99 years emerges in both images and names during the vehicular chase, when, after the second robbery is aborted, Dog Head and colleagues track the movements of Shan and his gang. Having recognized that there is a man behind the gang, the IB police unit gives him the name "The Hollow Man", a reference to T. S. Eliot's poem *The Hollow Men*. The choice articulates what their hybrid speech, which intermixes English words with a Hong Kong Cantonese dialect, has already been indicating — that British culture continues to participate in contemporary Hong Kong. Moreover, the legacy of British hegemony is readable through the city that is mapped by Shan's and the IB's movements. Racing through the city, while receiving reports from the station by those monitoring surveillance cameras, the policing trajectory informs us of street names through which Shan has passed. Here, the moving camera captures a city that has moved historically. Writing of Paris, which he refers to as "the *ville qui remue*, the city that is always on the move", Walter Benjamin points out that nevertheless, the city retains some aspects of stasis through its street names, which "preserve the name of a landed proprietor ... the movement of the streets [is thus constituted as] the movement of names".[9] Similarly, in the Hong Kong of *Eye in the Sky*, the continual displacement of historical provenances with new structures and expanding commerce nevertheless preserves vestiges of historical proprietary control. The metropolitan transit stations and streets passed in the IB police's pursuit of Shan — Jordan MTR (Mass Transit Railway) station, Nathan Road, Aberdeen Street, Staunton Street, Lyndhurst Terrace, and Pottinger Street — preserve the names of former British proprietors of the city state. Yet it is clear that Hong Kong, like the Paris observed by Benjamin, is in constant transformation as it, like all global cities, is continually shaped by the forces of global commerce.

Simultaneous with the time images of the contemporary and historical Hong Kong is the vocational time allocated to Piggy's character. In her first encounter with Dog Head, early in the film narrative, when he accosts her and says he recognizes her, Piggy fails to maintain her cover by hesitating in her denials of the identity that Dog Head is insisting on. Late in the film, Shan, who has the same keen visual memory as the IB policing operatives, accosts her in an eating establishment and insists that he recognizes her as someone who has been following him. This time, Piggy does not blow her cover, even though Shan knows that she is lying. And in yet another pair of related scenes, Piggy first fails to stick to her mission, instead stopping to help a downed policeman, but later, as the film's climax approaches, she acts more professionally, managing to leave a badly wounded Dog Head (who has been slashed in the neck by Shan) to continue her policing task.

---

9. The quotation is from Walter Benjamin's Notebook P of his Paris project. I have taken the passage from Samuel Weber's (2003, pp. 22-23) discussion of Benjamin's Paris.

Once Piggy is again on task, her new-found ability to focus leads to the capture and killing of Shan, the end of the gang's threat to local commerce, and to the promise of an effective career in law enforcement. However, in some ways we learn more from the impediments to Piggy's ultimate success. Because the main cops-and-robbers drama in *Eye in the Sky* proceeds in Hong Kong's commodity- and media-saturated environment, we are able to observe an articulation between two aspects of Hong Kong's participation in a modernization process, which is well described by Jonathan Crary (1995). First, it is evident that Hong Kong shares in the global modernizing process that involves "a ceaseless and self-perpetuating creation of new needs, new products, and new consumption". The second aspect involves rapid changes in "perceptual modalities", which are also produced by a modern capitalism that has increasingly "undermine[d] any stable or enduring structure of perception". Given "the emergence of a social, urban, psychic, industrial field, increasingly saturated with sensory input", attention has become one of modernity's primary problems. As Crary summarizes it, we can regard "one crucial aspect of modernity as a continual crisis of attention" (Crary 1999, p. 47).

Crary's observations speak directly to the notable moments of distraction in the film, two of which I have already noted with respect to *Eye in the Sky*'s robbery and policing tasks. One is Fat Man's sudden desire for a piece of chicken, which distracts him from his surveillance of the street during the robbery. Another is a distraction created by a street food and trinket seller, who interferes with the surveillance task of one of the police's street operatives, and another is the distraction created by the mortally wounded policeman, whose condition distracts Piggy from her pursuit of one of the crime culprits. However, while a shared need for the thieves and police to watch and time the rhythms of the city from panoptic vantage points is central to the film's drama, at the same time the film displays a more general aspect of modernity: the ways in which the multiple desire-provoking stimuli of the modern city inhibit or interfere with attention-demanding projects.

Georg Simmel's famous account of the psychic demands that the modern city levies on its inhabitants, especially for those unused to coping with urban sensoriums, remains influential:

> The rapid crowding of changing images, the sharp discontinuity in the grasp of a single glance, and the unexpectedness of onrushing impression. These are the psychological conditions which the metropolis creates. With each crossing of the street, with the tempo and multiplicity of economic, occupational and social life, the city sets up a deep contrast with small town and rural life with reference to the sensory foundations of modern life. (Simmel 1950, p. 410)[10]

However, we have to modify Simmel's formulation in two ways to attain a political grasp of the management of the city's hyperstimulating sensorium in *Eye In*

---

10. I take this quotation from a contemporary analysis of modernity's hyperstimuli (Singer 1995, p. 73), which acknowledges its debt to Simmel's original formulation of the phenomenon.

the Sky. The first alteration requires a shift from a psychological to an aesthetic idiom, so that the film's characters become aesthetic rather than psychological subjects. Treating cinematic subjects not as static entities with fixed personalities but as mobile beings with multiple possibilities for becoming shifts our attention from the motivational forces of individuals — from psychic subjectivity — to aesthetic subjects, to the ways that characters' interactions and trajectories of movement articulate spatio-temporal frames. Leo Bersani and Ulysse Dutoit enact such a conceptual shift in perspective in their reading of Jean-Luc Godard's film *Contempt* (1963), a film treating a couple that becomes estranged when the wife Camille (Bridget Bardot) changes her affect toward her husband Paul (Michel Piccoli) from love to contempt. They point out that Godard's concern is not for "the psychic origins of contempt" but for "its effects on the world". In the film, this concern is articulated through "what contempt does to cinematic space ... how it affect[s] the visual field within which Godard works, and especially the range and kinds of movement allowed for in that space" (Bersani & Dutoit 2004, p. 6). Similarly, what a critical, politically oriented reading of Yau Nai-Hoi's *Eye in the Sky* can provide is not insight into the motivations of robbers and police detectives but into the way that both robbery and policing render a cinematic articulation of the spatial history and temporal rhythms of Hong Kong.

The second shift requires us to modify Simmel's general ascription of the mental life of the city by recognizing that different characters face different levels of demand for stimulus management and a general rendering of the city as legible. In *Eye in the Sky*, the costs of inattention weigh heavily on the personae involved in robbery and policing and, further, have different consequences depending on a character's level in each hierarchical organization. Moreover, a recognition that attentiveness to signs and stimuli has differential implications for different types can lead us to a more general consideration of the micropolitics of contemporary global cities. For example, the consequences of ignoring surveillance technologies can produce disastrous consequences for illegal aliens and bad, but less disastrous, ones for shoplifters. And if instead of focusing on illegal acts and structures of policing, one instead treats levels of estrangement within the city, we can access a kind of micropolitics of everyday life that pertains to Hong Kong, Berlin, and all global cities. For example, sensitive to the micropolitics of adjustment afflicting immigrants in large global cities, the artist Krzysztof Wodiczko has invented technological prostheses for them to wear. One is an "alien staff", which resembles a biblical shepherd's rod. It carries a video monitor at its top that runs visuals and voices of the carrier's biography. The device is meant to overcome the anonymity of the immigrant as well as to disrupt the practices of inattention that distance people from each other in public space. As Wodiczko (1999, p. 104) puts it: "As the small image on the screen may attract attention and provoke observers to come very close to the monitor and therefore to the operator's face, the usual distance between the stranger and the observer will decrease". Whatever may be the ultimate effects of the interactions provoked by Wodiczko's various devices, his approach to modern urbanism articulates a recognition of the differential costs of urban attentiveness and inattentiveness.

However, if we return to the specific problematic that *Eye in the Sky*'s cops-and-robbers scenario enacts, we are encouraged to ascend to an identity problematic that afflicts Hong Kong as a whole and consider a collective identity issue — the problem of Chineseness. That issue becomes apparent if we recognize that for all the dynamics that *Eye in the Sky*'s *mise en scène* lends to Hong Kong — the changes evident in the city's built environment, its culinary practices, global commercial outlets that seem to be displacing the traditional street commerce, and the ongoing hide-and-seek dramas involving robbery and policing — there are significant aspects of cultural resistance accompanying those dynamics. To retrieve that cultural resistance, we can recast the two culinary events to which I refer above — one in which policing is interrupted when a police captain says that it is "time for soup" and the other when the gang's fighting ends with the injunction "Let's barbecue!" — as moments in which a traditional Chinese culinary habitus remains in a city that is otherwise too drawn into global commerce to provide time and space for traditional Chinese culture.

Once we discern such moments of arrest in an otherwise hyperkinetic drama and setting, we have to question what exactly is being policed by Hong Kong's IB unit. Recalling the earlier quotation about the importance of policing in a rapidly shifting Hong Kong, that "the Hong Kong police survive as guardians of the territories' political stability and cultural identity", Yau's *Eye in the Sky* ascends from a crime story involving simply a politics of crime and punishment to a politics of cultural governance with the IB police unit as the primary governing agent. Clearly, the police are the significant *who* with respect to the subject of governance. However, to discern the object or the *what* of that governance, one has to recognize the peculiarities of Hong Kong's relationship with Chineseness. As Kwai-Cheung Lo characterizes it:

> Hong Kong's Chineseness is a site of performative contradictions. Its existence is simply a living and contingent contradiction, in the sense that the city's culture both exaggerates and negates Chineseness in the vicissitudes of its sociopolitical milieu [as a result] Hong Kong culture operates as an articulation of "transitional Chineseness". (Lo 2005, p. 4)

Accordingly, the role of policing in Hong Kong is to maintain Hong Kong's status as, in Lo's (2005, p. 6) terms, "the master signifier of the Chinese nation". Within such a context, crime becomes a signifier that exceeds its threat to the commercial enterprises it preys upon. As Lo (2005, p. 6) points out, the Hong Kong enclave, with its notorious drugs, prostitution, and gangs, among other things, has been regarded by the governmental leadership in China as an affront to "traditional Chinese moral values". And as a representative of the bad and corrupt *vis-à-vis* the good of the mainland, Hong Kong has served to reinforce China's moral identity with its very transgressions. Thus, the policing response to the Shan gang's robberies can be construed as a policing-while-highlighting of the rampant anti-Chineseness that constitutes Hong Kong's difference from mainland China. The film's presentation of the need for a surveillant policing in Hong Kong thus serves as a warrant of Chineseness, giving an extended (if ironic) meaning to the sense in which the cinematic representations of Hong Kong's police (and Shan's gang for that matter) serve to protect Chinese cultural identity, even as it shows that culture is in a state of transition. Yau's crime story therefore devolves into a complex cultural governance story and encourages, once again, a reflection on the intercity cinematic experience with which my analysis begins, because politics in contemporary Berlin is very much about cultural governance, which, in the case of Berlin, involves how to represent Germanness.

Conclusion: Back to Berlin

While *Eye in the Sky*'s foregrounding of policing and its scenes of Hong Kong's culinary culture speak to a politics of Chinese identity, cultural governance in my viewing venue, Berlin, is articulated through the arts in general and architecture especially. While contemporary Hong Kong cinema is one of the primary genres within which the city's Chinese identity is thought and negotiated, especially since the transfer from British to Chinese control (cf. Cieko 2006), the negotiation of Berlin's participation in the issue of Germanness has been centered on the architectural projects though which Berlin has sought to transcend its troubled past. Given that collective identity involves the temporal projections of memory, and further that the cogency of such projections requires visible markings, the creation of the new Berlin has proceeded with the presumption that "memory is built" (Till 2005, p. 17). As a result, the process of designing the built environment of the city has involved a "negotiated politics of memory" (ibid.), which has intensified in Berlin since the Berlin Wall came down and the capital was transferred to Berlin from Bonn. Indeed, as Andreas Huyssen (2003, p. 51) puts it: "there is no other western city that bears the marks of twentieth century history as intensely and self-consciously as Berlin".

While Hong Kong architecture often proceeds through the establishment of monuments to its past — for example, the declaration as a monument of Flagstaff House, once a British military headquarters and now a museum — Berlin's architecture is self-consciously anti-monumental (Huyssen 2003). Thus, Norman Foster's Reichstag emphasizes transparency and accessibility in order to articulate a democratic present in contradistinction to Speer's monumentalism, which was meant to project authority with seemingly impenetrable facades. As Huyssen suggests, the historical distancing impetus of contemporary Berlin architecture proceeds within the binary of the visible—invisible (Huyssen 2003, p. 7), so that the built environment articulates a progressively-oriented history of space. Thus, debate over how to shape the new Berlin is concerned with superseding the past and convincing Germany, as well as the rest of the world, that the new Germanness is emancipated from previous versions. Therefore, my viewing situation — watching the rapidly mutating, hyperkinetic Hong Kong of Yau's *Eye in the Sky* while situated in a rapidly and self-consciously changing Berlin — ultimately provoked a consideration of modes of cultural governance in the modern global city and the genres through which they are articulated.

References

Abbas, A. (1997) *Hong Kong: Culture and the Politics of Disappearance*, University of Minnesota Press, Minneapolis, MN.
Abbas, A. (1999) 'Hong Kong: Other Histories, Other Politics', *Public Culture*, vol. 9, no. 3, pp. 293-313.
Bell, D. & Valentine, G. (1997) *Consuming Geographies*, Routledge, New York.
Benjamin, W. (1968) 'On Some Motifs in Baudelaire', in *Illuminations*, trans. Zohn, H., Schocken Books, New York.
Bersani, L. & Dutoit, U. (2004) *Forms of Being: Cinema, Aesthetics, Subjectivity*, British Film Institute, London.
Bordwell, D. (2000) *Planet Hong Kong: Popular Cinema and the Art of Entertainment*, Harvard University Press, Cambridge, MA.
Bordwell, D. (2002) 'Film Futures', *SubStance*, vol. 31, no. 1, pp. 88-104.
Bruno, G. (2002) *Atlas of Emotion: Journeys in Art, Architecture, and Film*, Verso, New York.
Burgin, V. (2004) *The Remembered Film*, Reaktion Books, London.
Cieko, A. T. (2006) 'Hong Kong: Cinematic Cycles of Grief and Glory', in Cieko, A. T. (ed.), *Contemporary Asian Cinema*, Berg Publishers, New York, pp. 169-181.
Crary, J. (1999) *Suspensions of Perception: Attention, Spectacle, and Modern Culture*, MIT Press, Cambridge, MA.
Deleuze, G. (1986) *Cinema 1*, trans.Tomlinson, H. & Habberjam, B., University of Minnesota Press, Minneapolis, MN.
Deleuze, G. (1989) *Cinema 2*, trans.Tomlinson, H. & Galeta, R., University of Minnesota Press, Minneapolis, MN.
Deleuze, G. (1992) 'Postscript on the Societies of Control', *October*, no. 59, pp. 3-7.
Dimendberg, E. (2004) *Film Noir and the Spaces of Modernity*, Harvard University Press, Cambridge, MA.
Doane, M. A. (2002) *The Emergence of Cinematic Time*, Harvard University Press, Cambridge, MA.
Fang, K. (2003) 'Britain's Finest: The Royal Hong Kong Police', in Burton, M., *After the Imperial Turn*, Duke University Press, Durham, NC, pp. 292-307.
Foucault, M. (1986) 'Of Other Spaces', *Diacritics*, vol. 16, no. 1, pp. 22-27.
Guy, S. (2004) 'Shadow Architectures: War, Memories, and Berlin's Futures', in Graham, S. (ed.), *Cities, War and Terrorism: Towards an Urban Geopolitics*, Blackwell, Cambridge, MA.
Haxthausen, C. W. (1990) '"A New Beauty": Ernst Ludwig Kirchner's Images of Berlin', in Haxthausen, C. W. & Suhr, H. (eds), *Berlin: Culture and Metropolis*, University of Minnesota Press, Minneapolis, MN, pp. 58-94.
Huyssen, A. (2003) *Present Pasts: Urban Palimpsests and the Politics of Memory*, Stanford University Press, Stanford, CA.
King, A. (2006) 'Postcolonial Cities, Post Colonial Critiques', in Berking, H., Frank, S., Frers, L., Low, M., Meier, L., Steets, S. & Stoetzer, S. (eds), *Negotiating Urban Conflicts*, Transcript Verlag, Bielefeld.
Kramer, J. (1999) 'Living with Berlin', *The New Yorker*, July 5th, pp. 84-92.
Leach, W. (1993) *Land of Desire*, Pantheon, New York.
Leon, D. (2002) *Wilful Behavior*, William Heinemann, New York.
Lo, K.-C. (2005) *Chinese Face/Off: The Transnational Popular Culture of Hong Kong*, University of Illinois Press, Champaign, IL.
Ma, K. (2001) 'Consuming Satellite Modernities', *Cultural Studies*, vol. 15, no. 3-4, pp. 444-463.
Rancière, J. (2004) *The Politics of Aesthetics*, trans. Rockhill, G., Continuum, New York.

Simmel, G. (1950) 'The Metropolis and Mental Life', in Wolff, K. H. (ed.), *The Sociology of Georg Simmel*, Free Press, New York.

Singer, B. (1995) 'Modernity, Hyperstimulus, and the Rise of Popular Sensationalism', in Charney, L. & Schwartz, V. R. (eds), *Cinema and the Invention of Modern Life*, University of California Press, Berkeley, CA.

Strathhausen, C. (2003) 'Uncanny Spaces: The City in Ruttmann and Vertov', in Shiel, M. & Fitzmaurice, T. (eds), *Screening the City*, Verso, New York.

Stokes, L. & Hoover, M. (1999) *City on Fire: Hong Kong Cinema*, Verso, New York.

Taylor, P. (2000) 'World Cities and Territorial States under Conditions of Contemporary Globalization', *Political Geography*, vol. 19, no. 1, pp. 5-32.

Till, K. (2005) *The New Berlin: Memory, Politics, Place*, University of Minnesota Press, Minneapolis, MN.

Virilio, P. (1991) *The Aesthetics of Disappearance*, Semiotext(e), New York.

Weber, S. (2003) '"Streets, Squares, Theaters": A City on the Move — Walter Benjamin's Paris', *Boundary 2*, vol. 30, no. 1, pp. 17-30.

Wesemann, E. (2000) *Film Museum of Berlin: The Exhibition*, Nicolai, Berlin.

Wise, M. (1999) 'The New Berlin: Expressing Government Power with Pomposity', *The New York Times on the Web*, http://www/com/yr/mo/day/art;leisure/berlin-architecture.htm (accessed 2 December 2000).

Wodiczko, K. (1999) *Critical Vehicles*, The MIT Press, Cambridge, MA.

Zukin, S. (1992) 'Postmodern Urban Landscapes', in Lash, S. & Friedman, J. (eds), *Modernity and Identity*, Blackwell, Cambridge, MA.

Index

Page numbers in **Bold** represent figures.

Abbas, A. 71, 104–5
Africa 59–60, 71–6; Africanness 71–3; cultures of expression 64; farm 60, 63–4; housing estates 65; modern African 62, 71–3; modes of life 61; polyrhythmia 71; postcolonial 73; rhythmanalysis 70–5; Sheng-speaking 75–6; socialism 62; violence 72
African Metropolis (Hake) 65
Africanness 71–3
Aguilar Branch Public Library 43–5
Aguilar, G. 44
Aitkins, S. 92–3
Akira (comic book series) 12
Aldrich, R. 27
Altman, R. 26
American Ruins (Vergara) 53
animation 12
anime 12–13
Appadurai, A.: and Holston, J. 68
architecture 5–10, 12–13, 24
Arendt, H.: modernity 30; private *vs.* public matters 30–3, 36
artistic practice 12

Babel (Iñárritu) 4, 10–11, 16–17; Chieko 10, **11**, 16–17; digital space 10
Bachelard, G. 62
Bakhtin, M.M. 82; chronotopes 93; eroticism 90; heteroglossia 82; novels 94
Barthes, R. 101
Baudelaire, C. 15–16
Bell, D.: and Valentine, G. 110
Benjamin, W. 15–16, 25, 99–100, 113
Berlant, L. 92–3
Berlin: cinematic quality 103; cinematic treatment 101; geopolitical framing 101; Neue Nationalgalerie 102; Potsdamer Platz 100
Berlin Film Festival 99–100
Berman, M. 68

Bhabha, H. 56, 68
Blixen, K. 59–66, 69; African farm 63–4, 69; authentic African 61; house 63
Bloch, E. 10; digital revolution 10
Bois, Y.A. 5, 24
Bordwell, D. 108
Bosire, M. 75
Boston in *Mystic River* 83–96; architecture 95; cinematography 85; Flats (blue-collar area) 86; imagined borders 88; Last Drop (bar located in the Flats) 88; neighbourhood 85; police 85; racial/spatial order 89; Red Sox games 85; small communities 85; suburbs 85–6; working-class 94
Boyle, Dave 81–5, 87, 91–3; and Markum, Jimmy **95**; murders 83; reputation 87; urban anxieties 84; victim 92
Bronx 39
Brown, B.J. 3–17, 121
Bruno, G. 5–7, 10, 15–17, 24, 100; cinematic process 7; *haptic space* 7; sight-seeing 16
Burch, N. 86
The Business (Rodriguez) 49

Caché (Haneke) 21–5, 27–37; architecture 24, 34; familial space **33**; flashback sequences 22–3; home space 25, 27–30, 33; Laurent, Georges *see* Laurent, Georges; Majid *see* Majid; opening shot sequences 21, 23; reverse-rewind shots 23–4; scenes 28–9
Carey, P. 12
Celluloid Skyline (Sanders) 82
Central Park North, East Harlem 54
Certeau, M. de 64
Chicken and Duck Talk (Yu and Ko) 104
child's perspective 4
Chinese decorations 51
Chinese families: East Harlem 43–4
Chirac, J. 19–20; development 20
cinema 15–17; history 101; narrational space 17
cinematic technique 17

INDEX

Columina, B. 28–9, 34–5
comic book series: *Akira* 12
Contempt (Godard) 115
Coppola, S. 3–8, 17
Crary, J. 114

Daniels, L.A. 48
Dassin, J. 90
Dawnay Day (investment bank) 54
De La Vega, J. 55; art 55
Deleuze, G. 24, 26, 96, 101; and Guattari, F. 73–4
Devine, Sean 81–5, 86–7, 89, 91–3; mediator 91–2; State Homicide detective 84, 86–7, 91; urban anxieties 91
Dickens, C. 36
digital revolution 10
digital space 10
Dimendberg, E. 84, 107
Dinesen, G. 60
Dirty Pretty Things (Frear) 26
Doane, M.A. 112

East Harlem 39–41; 6-train 39; affordable housing 47; architectural changes 45; Central Park North 54; Chinese families 43–4; community of immigrants 46; crime rates 56; Dawnay Day (investment bank) 54; diverse community 40–1; economic changes 53; economic revival 49; El Barrio 40; families 41; geography 40; home 41; housing projects 45–7; hybridity 56; immigrant groups 48; inhabitants 55; Japanese neighbours 52–3; La Esperanza Homes *see* La Esperanza Homes (East Harlem); Latino groups 40; migration patterns 48; Puerto Rican immigrants 40–2, 44; racial tensions 53; rapid change 55–6; revival 43; rising cost of living 56; Spanish Harlem 40; subway line 40; veteran residents 56
East Harlem housing development 47–50; buildings 48; residents 48; staircases 49–50
Eisenstein, S.M. 5, 24, 81
El Barrio 40
Elhadad, L.: and Payeur, P. 25–6
eroticism 90
Eye in the Sky (Nai-Hoi) 103, 105–17; Chan Chong Shan 106–9, **107**, 113–14; Dog Head 106–9, 113–14; eating scene 111; Fat Man 109–10, 114; forking-path plots 108–9; Piggy 106–9, **107**, 113–14; robbery 112; surveillance regime 106–7

Fang, K. 105, 108
Fanon, F. 70
Foucault, M. 20, 72

France: borders 20; immigration 20–6; multicultural 26
Frear, S. 26
French family 32, 36
Fuller, S. 105–6

Gallagher, B. 19–37, 121
Godard, J.L. 115
Gosford Park (Altman) 26
The Grave of the Fireflies (Takahata) 12
Guattari, F.: and Deleuze, G. 73–4
Guy, S. 100

Hake, A. 65
Haneke, M. 21–5, 27–37; Paris 25
haptic space 5–7, 17
Harlem 39
Harris, Bob 5–6; bodily comportment 7, 16; experience of Tokyo 8; lived space 6; physiognomy **8**; relationship with Charlotte 6–7, 15–16
Hayden, D. 8–9, 52; De La Vega's art 55; urban landscapes 43
Highmore, B. 11–12, 71, 82
Holston, J.: and Appadurai, A. 68
home space: *Caché* (Haneke) 25, 26–30, 33; media space 34
Hong Kong 100–1; architecture 104; Chineseness 116; contemporary 105; culinary culture 109–11; historical time 112; local culture 104; police 108; vocational commitments 108
Hoover, M.: and Stokes, L. 104
Howard, E. 69
Huyssen, A. 117

Iñárritu, A.G. 4, 10–11, 16–17
The Invention of Africa (Mudimbe) 61

Japanese adaption 11
Japanese neighbours: East Harlem 52–3
Japanese novel 14
Jordan, J. 45, 57

Karengata 61–2
Karp, I.: and Lavine, S.D. 63
Kenya: urban revolution 65
Kibwana, K.: and Mituallah, W. 70
Kincaid, J.: home 41
Kirchner, E.L. 102–3; *Potsdamer Platz* 103
Kittler, F. 43
Ko, C.: and Yu, R. 104
Korang, K.L. 74
Kramer, J. 104
Krause, L.: and Petro, P. 13
Kurtz, R. 65–6
Kyoto: tourist attractions 13

INDEX

La Esperanza Homes (East Harlem) 49–53; Chinese decorations 51; differing aesthetic tastes 51; diverse families 50–1; garden 51; Japanese neighbours 52–3; luxury 50; ownership 50; red bricks 50
La Haine 36
Lancelin, A.: and Vigoureux, E. 27
Landler, M. 27
Landmarks - A Permanent Exhibition (Payeur and Elhadad) 25–6
Lasswell, H.D. 83
Laurent, Georges 21–2; Anne (his wife) 21–3; axe 22; bedroom 35; childhood home 28; familial space 33; and Majid 22, 30–1; private *vs.* public matters 30–2; public visibility 31; surveillance footage 21–3, 29; talk-show set 32–3
Lavine, S.D.: and Karp, I. 63
Le Corbusier 34–5; architecture 34–5; houses 35
Le Pen, J.M. 19–20
Leach, W. 6; theatrical strategies 6
Lefebvre, H. 71, 75; triangle 91–4
Lehane, D. 81–4, 89–90, 93
Leon, D. 110–11
Lloyd Parry, R. 8–9
Lo, K.C. 116
Loos, A. 34–5; architecture 34–5; home space 34; Moller House 35
Lopez, J. 39
Los Angeles: vernacular architecture 9
Lost in Translation (Coppola) 3–8, 17; Charlotte 6–7, 15–16; depiction (ontological connections) 5; *haptic* space 5–7; Harris, Bob *see* Harris, Bob; karaoke performances 11; life 8; opening sequence 5; primary venue 6

Ma, K. 111
Maasai Progress Plan (Tanzanian government) 62
Maasai way of life 62–3
McCann, E. 87, 91–2
Macgoye, M.O. 66–7; poetics of everyday life 67–8
Majid 22–3; and Georges 22, 30–1; social invisibility 31; suicide 23, 29–30
Manga (Hokusai) 12–13
Markum, Jimmy 81–5, 87, 91–3; and Boyle, Dave **95**; criminality 87; family 89; Marita (first wife) 89–90; reputation 87; urban utopia 83
Mason, P. 70
Mayol, P. 70
Mazrui, A.A. 62
Mbembe, A.: and Nuttall, S. 71
media space: home space 34

Miller, D.A. 36–7
Mituallah, W.: and Kibwana, K. 70
Moller House 35
Momma Roma (Pasolini) 95–6; aesthetic orientation 96
Moretti, F. 66
Mudimbe, V.Y. 61
Mumford, L. 73, 86, 90
Mungiki militia 72
Muoroto and Kibagare demolitions (informal settlements) 70
Murakami, H. 14
Mystic River 81–4, 81–96, 89–90, 93; aesthetic orientation 96; Boston *see* Boston in *Mystic River*; Boyle, Dave *see* Boyle, Dave; Devine, Sean *see* Devine, Sean; genre 89; Katie's murder 86–9, 93; Markum, Jimmy *see* Markum, Jimmy; urban space 82

Nai-Hoi, Y. 103, 105–17
Nairobi 65–70; collective assemblage 70; green city 69; hidden 67; Muoroto and Kibagare demolitions 70; post-colonial 65–8; Pumwani 69; urban culture 70
The Naked City (Dassin) 90
Nangulu-Ayuku, A. 69
National Center of the History of Immigration (Paris) 25–6
Neue Nationalgalerie, Berlin 102
New York City: residential areas 52
Nuttall, S.: and Mbembe, A. 71

Oliver Twist (Dickens) 36
On the 6 (Lopez) 39
Opondo, S.O. 59–76, 121
Out of Africa (Blixen) 59–60, 64, 69

Pan, A. 39–57, 121; father 52; life events 43
Paris: city space 37; French culture 26; geopolitical space of racial class tensions 20; urban city 23, 25
Pasolini 95–6
Payeur, P.: and Elhadad, L. 25–6
Petro, P.: and Krause, L. 13
Pickup on South Street (Fuller) 105–7, **106**; surveillance regime 106–7
poems 66–8
politics 21, 42
Potsdamer Platz, Berlin 100
Potsdamer Platz (Kirchner) 103, **103**
Puerto Rican immigrants: East Harlem 40–2, 44

Rancière, J. 21, 74, 108–9; art 42–3; politics 42, 74
Red Sox games: Boston 85

INDEX

Rhodes, J.D. 95–6
Rodriguez, J. 46; local businesses, East Harlem 46–7; photographs 46, 49
Roppongi, Tokyo 9–10
Rossiter, J. 54
Rowe, N. 81–96, 121
Rybczynski, W. 41

Said, E. 62–3, 67
Sanders, J. 82
Sands, P. 10
Sarkozy, N. 25
Sassen, S. 41, 54; global cities 55
Scarry, E. 94
Schneider, L. 62
Shapiro, M.J. 1, 99–117, 121; seminar on research methods 1
Sharman, R. 40, 42; East Harlem residents 42, 44, 47, 49, 52; racial tensions East Harlem 53
Sheng-speaking 75–6
Shizuko Akashi (Murakami) 14
Silverman, K. 29
Simmel, G. 8, 114; life 8
A Slow Boat to China (Murakami) 14–15
Smoke (Wang and Auster) 21–2
socialism: Africa 62
Song of Nyarloka (Macgoye) 66–9
Spanish Harlem 40
Speer, A. 104
Steiner House 35
Stokes, L.: and Hoover, M. 104

Strathhausen, C. 101

Tanzanian government 62
The Tenants of East Harlem (Sharman) 42
theatrical strategies 6
Theory of Film Practice (Burch) 86
Thiong'o, N. wa 60
Till, K. 117
Tokyo 3–17; cityscape 13; filmic reflection 11; foreigners 9; inhabitants 9; international visitors 10; lived space 10; modern 13; panoramas 7; Roppongi 9–10; sense-memory 3; Uguisudani 9; urban 3–4, 13–14
Tyler, S. 66–7

Valentine, G.: and Bell, D. 110
Vergara, C.J. 53
Vidler, A. 25
Vigoureux, E.: and Lancelin, A. 27
Virilio, P. 101

White, H. 68
Wieviorka, M. 27
Wirth, L. 68–9, 73
Wirth-Nesher, H. 66
Wodiczko, K. 115

Yu, R.: and Ko, C. 104

Zukin, S. 104